TODD STRUNK

The Other Cancer Survivor

The Other Cancer Survivor

© 2022 Todd Strunk

Print ISBN: 978-1-66783-118-3
eBook ISBN: 978-1-66783-119-0

Dedication

This book is dedicated to my son, Tucker.

Always remember, Son that your Mom wanted nothing more than to beat cancer so she could be a part of your life. Not just life's milestones—your first lost tooth, your driver's license, graduation from high school, marriage—but the regular simple days, too—when you come home from school and you're tired, or when you score points in your game. She wanted to be there to cheer you on. Her biggest struggle was letting go and not being a part of your life after she passed.

Always remember. She loved you with her entire being.

Contents

Foreword

TIME HAS A WAY OF mixing events in the mind. For many weeks I felt a need to chronicle the events that surrounded my wife's illness and passing, not just to set things straight in my mind, but also for my son Tucker who was a little boy when everything took place. As the years have passed, I haven't always talked about why I did or didn't do something that affected his life. I just did it. What began as only a few pages, a simple narrative, has morphed into much more. In this process, I referenced a friend or someone that I knew and then later said I had no friends. This needs clarification.

For a person to become a true, close friend, you go through stages in a relationship. You begin as acquaintances. This is a person you recognize because you've seen them before or held a conversation with them. As the relationship progresses, you spend time together having a meal or sharing a recreational activity. Are you really friends at this point? You might think you are, but as time goes by, you don't develop the relationship further. Contrast this with a person who becomes a true friend. The relationship develops deeper and deeper. This person becomes the go-to person who will meet you at the park on a Saturday afternoon for a BBQ and some frisbee time or stop by just to watch the game. The relationship continues to deepen when that person drops everything to help you in your hour of need and vice versa.

Over the last decade I have had many people who have entered my life only to drift away after a few weeks or a couple of months. At the time, I felt like they were my friend. I was trying to deepen and develop our relationship, but because of circumstances we are no longer in communication. They have become, once again, an acquaintance even though I refer to them in this document as a friend.

Over the last decade, I have reconnected with two old Army buddies with whom I am in constant contact. When we are physically together, there is much laughter, but we live thousands of miles apart. This makes an afternoon at the park a difficult thing to accomplish. Over the last few years, I have made friends with a couple of nice ladies who have also lost loved ones due to cancer. We sit together at church for mutual protection. No one wants to be singled out, but we don't go hunting or fishing and haven't been to a hockey game together. We will gather for the holidays and celebrate with a meal and an exchange of gifts. They are my closest friends. Recently when I had covid, they made sure I had an ample supply of cookies to see me through my illness. When I talk about my friends today, these are the people in my life. None were present for the first two years after my wife passed away. Slowly our friendships have grown deeper.

This literary work is about friendship. When I lost my best friend to cancer, I needed someone who would be in my life and be my friend. What I got was many people I thought were my friends but left our relationship. Those people have been replaced with these four individuals who are amazing people in that they value me as much as I value them and our shared friendships.

This book has been edited by Brenda Brewer. She is that special person that lives inside the tense relationship between nouns and verbs. Without her help and guidance this literary work could never have happened. Thank you so much Brenda

Support

Let's Start at the Beginning

"You can expect that all the people who have been supporting you these last few months will drift away, and you'll find that your support network pretty much doesn't exist."

It had been about two hours since the end of my wife's memorial service. I had just stood at the head of a long, long line and spent the better part of an hour and a half greeting many of those in attendance and had only begun to get my wits about me. I had taken time to change my clothes and thank some of the people who were working so hard behind the scenes. I was enjoying the warmth of the fall sun. I was comfortable in jeans and a T-shirt, and a gentle breeze drifted across the parking lot outside my church. I was emotionally and physically exhausted. Wasted. Worn out. Just standing near my friend's car was taking all the emotional and physical drive I could muster. I just wanted to lie down and sleep. A deep exhaustion was setting in. Months of effort living at a full sprint each day had caught up to me and was overtaking my person entirely. In my mind, I kept thinking this was all just a bad dream, and if I could get a nap and rest a little and clear my head, then I would be able to return to reality and think clearly, but thinking clearly wasn't really an option for me at the moment. If I had been able to think clearly, I probably would have run away screaming at the top of my lungs. I was operating in a thick emotional fog that wouldn't clear for months, so what my closest friend was telling me really didn't sink in like it should have. It would take about four months before I fully understood what that statement meant.

As I walked to my car nearby, the thought gently drifted through my mind: *Well now maybe things will return to normal.* Normal? What exactly is normal? Let's just say I wasn't prepared for the paradigm shift my life had just taken. Let me be honest here, it's been eight years at this writing, and I'm only now beginning to understand how things have changed, but to fully understand that, I guess I should start at the beginning, way back three years before, when things had been "normal."

Round One

It was an average evening. We had had an average day. My son Tucker had been at daycare, and my wife Sheryl had been at her work. I was enjoying an evening at home. Being a high school teacher, I spend some evenings at work announcing a sporting event or coaching or supporting students in many different ways. So, for me an evening home with my family was a perfect way to end the day. When Sheryl and Tucker arrived home, I was able to play with Tucker for about an hour before dinner. We might have played with cars or watched some children's TV. At the same time Sheryl would have prepared dinner. A stereotypical American family evening.

As things progressed that night, I was in the bedroom folding laundry, snapping towels, and making sure the T shirts were folded just so to ensure the creases would be square, a hold over habit from my military days. Sheryl was tickling Tucker as he lay on the bed. Because he was only two, she wasn't very concerned when his feet got close to her chest. After all, how much damage can a two-year-old do?

Keep in mind Sheryl was pretty tough. When Tucker was born, she willed herself to not give into the pain. She would eventually ask for some pain meds, but the epidural didn't sit correctly against the spine, so she mostly gave birth without the assistance of any pain meds. On this particular night, when she let out a yelp and began crying, I knew something was very wrong.

The next morning, I told Sheryl to be sure to make an appointment with the doctor. Initially she dismissed the idea, but I insisted that she see a doctor. She did make the appointment, but simply dismissed the pain. The doctor told her that a bruise would form, so she should look for a black and blue mark in a few weeks. Six weeks later the bruise still hadn't manifested. I began to get alarmed when she asked me to feel for a lump just a couple of inches below her collarbone on the right side of her chest. The next day she called the doctor and explained the situation and that she could now feel a lump. The doctor's office scheduled an appointment for the next day. No more excuses. Tests were ordered and exams were given. The diagnosis was stage two breast cancer with a lymphoma component. The cancer wasn't just in the tumor but had spread to the lymph system, too. The doctor recommended surgery with follow-on treatment of chemotherapy and radiation. Things began to happen fast–too fast. For six weeks we'd been put on hold. It's nothing to worry about. It's just a bruise. These things happen–blah blah blah. Now it was surgery on my wife within 72 hours of our first feeling that lump.

My life became condensed. My mental state was such that I could really only see things down a long black tunnel. I would wake up each day longing to see a small light flickering at the end of that tunnel. A heaviness hung over me like I was carrying a dentist's radiation shield. A lead ball filled my stomach, and heartburn was a constant. I found myself clenching my jaw and would have to try and unclench it to make the ache go away as I was trying to push through the stress of the situation. I was feeling the physical results of having a wife battling cancer, but I tried to keep it all to myself. After all, why should I complain, I wasn't the person with cancer.

As we told people about what was happening, we both noticed something. People want to make you feel good. We talked about it many times during those first nine months. Empty phrases came with the hopes we would find peace. At the same time, those who had been through similar trials were able to reassure us, not with empty phrases, but solid statements that we could lean on for comfort. We began to reevaluate how we answered people. Words became much more important.

We entered a time measured in chemo treatments and the times in between. Chemo day was Thursday, and Sheryl would spend the entire morning at each appointment. Arriving home after her first treatment, I asked her how it went.

"I was clearly the new guy," she said, "I was the only patient with hair." Because of the strength of her treatment, it took just a couple of days for her to begin to lose her hair. We talked about what and how she wanted to deal with cancer and her treatments which we figured would be worse than the disease. I suggested a bright breast cancer pink mohawk. The pink represented her struggle against the disease. The mohawk represented her fierce warrior attitude that she was using to defeat cancer. She was going to FLAG! Fight Like A Girl! I had been cutting my son's hair for a couple of years, so I offered my skills to help her obtain the mohawk. Because we had to bleach her light brown hair bright white and then re-dye it pink, the haircut took us a couple of hours, but she was proud of her new look. Checking out her new look in the mirror she proudly proclaimed, "I won't be the new guy next time I have chemo!"

Something interesting happened as a result of the crazy pink mohawk. People at work and church who would normally not have much to say to her suddenly became very interested in what was happening. The bright pink mohawk broke the ice and allowed conversation to happen. It usually started with a question like, "Why would you do that to your hair?" The response was usually something like, "Well it's going to fall out anyway, so why not have some fun with it while I can?" And the conversation was off and running. Mechanics from her work who would normally never talk to the lady from the office suddenly became interested and began to offer encouragement as she passed their workstation out in the mechanics' shop. The barista at our favorite coffee shack made a number of cars wait while he asked question after question about cancer and chemo. All of those questions began with a comment about the pink mohawk. Within just a few days all of her hair was gone, and she was completely bald, but people who knew her and had seen the mohawk would offer an encouraging comment, "Soon you'll be able to grow back that awesome pink mohawk."

The first set of drugs had a span of six hours before Sheryl began to feel ill. She found out on day one that she needed to be at home in her sweats and on the couch by the time that six hours was up or she was in real trouble. Yes, it made her very sick. The second treatment with this particular drug cocktail made her blood count drop to below one percent. The result was she would black out and collapse. This was cured by a simple shot and a few hours of rest, but the flu was nothing compared to chemo. The second drug had a longer span of 48 hours before it would take effect.

It was a Saturday morning, and Sheryl was still feeling pretty good. She was just waiting for the chemo to take effect. Between working when she could, being at the clinic for chemo, and sitting on the couch feeling like death warmed over, Sheryl hadn't been out for any relaxation in a few weeks. So, I loaded everyone in the truck. We stopped for a coffee and headed out for a long drive in the country. It was just an hour, but it was the break that she needed, a chance to relax and enjoy the beauty around us and not feel sick. It would become our regular routine during chemo. To this day, if I've had a particularly difficult week, I'll take a nice drive in the country while I enjoy a cup of coffee, and I'm ready for the next challenge.

After twenty weeks of chemo, it was time for radiation. Five days a week for nine weeks. It was the easiest part of the entire treatment plan. It was only a five-minute treatment, and the expected burning was only present the last couple of weeks. During radiation Sheryl began walking to regain stamina lost during chemo. Her first walk meant getting to the street and back to the front door. Soon her walks meant going all the way to the end of the block. Eventually we would get to a local park with nature trails where I would bring along a little red wagon so she could ride for a while when she was too tired to walk. Eventually the doctor pronounced her cured and gave her a schedule of appointments to make sure there wasn't any relapse. It had been a long year from the first sign of problems until radiation was complete, but it was past us.

Round Two

The next eighteen months were very routine. We would work during the work week and on Saturdays, and some Sundays we would have a family day. This meant a trip to a museum or the nearby zoo or a trip to the mountains for a day of tubing in the snow. These were good times. The pressure of the previous year was gone. We were working hard and playing almost as hard. I was given the opportunity to sell my prep period at work which meant that I would be making bonus pay every day. That helped pay down our expenses that had built up from cancer. We had many good memories during this eighteen-month break from cancer.

The last good day was a day spent at the ballpark. We arranged a sitter for Tucker, and we spent the day at an Oregon State Beavers Baseball game. We tailgated with some of my coworkers, and we all sat together in a group. It was a beautiful late April spring day in the Willamette Valley. As we headed home that evening, I asked Sheryl if she wanted anything to eat and offered to stop at our favorite burger stand.

"No I don't think so. I don't feel very good," she responded, "I'm kind of dizzy like I didn't get enough water to drink today." As I drove past the burger stand and headed for home, I apologized and told her I was sorry she didn't feel good. Within three weeks, that dizzy feeling would consume Sheryl.

It was the morning of Mother's Day, and at first, she thought she had food poisoning, but when no one else was sick from eating the same food, the poisoning idea was dismissed. Her condition worsened.

The first couple of weeks we thought that Sheryl had some other medical condition that made her dizzy. By dizzy, I don't mean just a little light-headed. This was crippling. Sheryl was continuously dizzy which caused her to feel like she had just stepped from a whirly-twirly amusement park ride. She would eat something soft like soup, and within a few minutes, it would come back up. One particular night, Sheryl woke up and began vomiting uncontrollably. After about 30 minutes of hearing her gag and vomit, I decided we were headed to the emergency room. It was amazing how fast we got a room to ourselves when Sheryl began retching while standing over the reception desk.

Throughout this five-week period of time, I had this deep sense of foreboding that I couldn't shake. It was just a presence that hung over me. No one from the medical community would order the proper test to check to see if cancer was present. It was frustrating to see my wife suffering and nothing really being done to solve the issue. Finally, we got word that an MRI would be performed on Sheryl's head.

Sheryl could hardly stand up straight let alone drive herself, and because a terminal illness hadn't been diagnosed, I was hard pressed to get time off from work, so her aunt drove her to the MRI. As she exited the MRI suite, the tech misspoke.

"I'm sure a doctor will be contacting you very soon to talk about the lesions on your brain."

"What do you mean *lesions*," my wife queried. Immediately the tech realized he had given away too much information and ushered my wife towards the exit, but we finally had word from someone that something really wrong was going on.

I was at work and just beginning my lunch break when I received a frantic call from Sheryl. The doctors had looked at the MRI and decided they wanted to perform a full body scan. Sheryl needed to be back at the MRI suite as soon as possible. It had taken five weeks of almost daily calls to the medical community trying to get a proper test to check for cancer. Now a second test was being ordered only 45 minutes after Sheryl had emerged from the first test in the MRI tube. The medical community was operating at full speed, and it was getting very scary. So, Sheryl called me and asked that I get to the clinic as soon as possible. Life had just begun to spin out of control.

It was nine o'clock on that same Friday night heading into Memorial Day weekend, that the phone rang. The call was from Los Angeles, California, a long way from our home in Salem, Oregon. When my wife took the call, I sat across the room and listened to the doctor explain how they had found lesions on the brain, and there were too many to count. A tumor was growing on the brain stem that was most likely causing the dizzy sensation. Along with the tumors on the brain, tumors were found in the lung and on the liver. The cancer had spread via the lymph system. Nine months of chemo and radiation had failed. Our world came to a complete halt, and I had to face the fact that I would soon be a single dad of a four-year-old boy. The dark presence that had been hanging over me the last five weeks now began to press on me and weigh me down. The paradigm was shifting.

At the same time Sheryl had family that was visiting from out of town, and the next morning we gathered for a big breakfast at my brother's house. Sheryl was getting tired and needed some rest, but Tucker was enjoying playing with his cousins, so he stayed and played while we went home for some rest and maybe talk about some end-of-life decisions we needed to consider. We had only just begun our conversation when the phone rang. Tucker had been hurt, and we needed to come over as quickly as we could. When we arrived, we found Tucker had two very badly scraped knees and a couple of bruises, but there were no tears. The story was that the cousins were playing outside in the back yard, and a giant swarm of bees flew just a few feet above the kids. The adults yelled for the kids to get inside, but Tucker was playing with a car, so emergencies would have to wait. This car needed to be parked. Knowing how quickly the situation could turn serious, my sister-in-law rushed across the yard and snatched Tucker up and headed inside, but she slipped when she reached the concrete patio. She went down, and so did Tucker. The result was that he had just a little bit of skin left on one knee. Because of the open wounds, he didn't want to bend his knees, so instead of walking, he waddled like a penguin. Normally this would make for a bad day and a few days of ointment and bandages, but our family was also working through the fact that Mom had just been diagnosed with terminal cancer. Things were spinning out of control and gaining speed.

The Portrait

As soon as Sheryl found out that the cancer had returned, she determined that we would need to have a family portrait taken. Brain surgery was scheduled immediately with the cancer diagnosis, so we needed to do that portrait on the same Saturday as the bee swarm incident. We had an appointment for that afternoon. Nothing was going to get in our way, not even a couple of scraped knees.

I parked the truck in the parking lot outside the mall that encompasses four blocks of our downtown business area. From the back seat I grabbed a diaper bag full of the things needed to keep a four-year-old occupied long enough to take some pictures. Then I grabbed the bag I was using for Sheryl. It had medicines and garbage bags for when she needed to vomit and some other items that we would need for our family portrait session. I then got my son out of the car and reached for my wife's hand to help her. Reality smacked me upside the head. Somehow, I needed to maneuver all of us and our things from the parkade to the photo studio, and I was the only one able to walk in a straight line. With a diaper bag slung across each shoulder, I wrapped an arm around my wife at the waist, my other arm around my son's shoulders, and we set off across the parking lot and into the first store and into an open mall area. We needed to get across the street on a pedestrian walkway and through another store to yet another open mall area where we would go down a flight of stairs. Once we reached the ground floor, we needed to travel the length of a city block to the photo studio. In total, we traveled over three city blocks and three streets and descended from the second level to the ground level. All the while, I was trying to steady not just my wife who was as steady as a drunk on a bender, but also half carrying my son who was wobbling along. We set off at a snail's pace, one foot in front of the other. Luckily, the stairs that descended from the second level to the first had a landing and I was able to get my son to the landing and return to the top of the stairs before my wife fell over. I was able to repeat the process for the bottom half of the stairs. After almost 20 minutes, we arrived at the photo studio.

What should have taken only a couple of hours turned into a four-hour ordeal. We retraced our steps back the way we had come reversing the process. Meanwhile in the back of my mind was dinner. People in our church had been providing us with meals now for over a month, and a family was set to bring over our evening meal except we were at the photo studio. Not to worry. They would set it outside on their front porch, and we could get it on our way home. As I bent down to pick up our meal, I realized that the roasted chicken had been sitting in the late afternoon sun for almost four hours. It was a warm sunny afternoon with the temperature hovering near seventy degrees. If we ate the chicken, it had the potential to make us very sick. I scooped up the meal and put it in the bed of the truck and decided we'd have pizza for dinner.

That Saturday was really when it all started. The life I had built was being torn down and reshaped. I had no control over what the outcome would be. I had always felt I could control things in my life. It was also the first day of living life under the umbrella of terminal cancer. The events of that day fully illustrate how someone going through a struggle of this magnitude really has no control over what takes place. They're just along for the ride. Five weeks earlier I had been pretty happy. I had a nice house on a small lot, and caring for my yard was a chore I took great pride in. I was bringing home extra pay each month. I had a pretty wife and young son who was always excited to go to daycare so he could feed the rabbits Cheetos, and we were trying for a second kid. Life was exactly where I wanted it to be. I was reaching my goals. What could go wrong? And that Saturday when I climbed out of bed, my goals were to spend the morning with family, visit the photo studio that afternoon, and relax that evening watching some television. I had not made the adjustment to the standard cancer time zone. I didn't plan on my son scraping up his knees. I didn't plan on the journey to the photo studio or four hours at the photo studio. Life suddenly wasn't going as planned. However, I still had tasks that needed completing. Laundry was still sitting on the floor in the hallway waiting to be sorted. Dinner dishes were still sitting in the sink. Baths needed to be administered. Life was still moving forward. I just had a new set of challenges to overcome.

That Saturday

I have always felt it was my responsibility as a husband to help my wife reach her goals, and I often set aside my goals to help my wife get things done. Until she got sick, she didn't need my help, but I did what I could to help her and to make her life easier. My mission was to support her however I could. I didn't know that on that Saturday supporting my wife would literally mean wrapping an arm around her waist and offering all my strength to support her so she could walk in a straight line without falling over. That particular Saturday has repeated itself many times over since 2013, maybe not in the same exact way but in some variation of life taking control and dictating how my time would be spent.

That Saturday night, completely exhausted from the ordeal of the day, I fell asleep on the couch. My wife woke me up crying because she couldn't reach a waste can to vomit in. So, before I could migrate from couch to bed, I needed to get her into a shower and cleaned up. I needed to wipe up the mess from the couch and the carpet, and then I needed to get caught up on all the other chores that I had put on hold for the day while we did pictures. I was beginning to lose sleep again like I had during chemo. The strain on my jaw as it clenched tighter and tighter was increasing. The all too familiar darkness was closing in. Only this time there was no light at the other end. We would spend the remainder of the weekend enjoying family time. We would plant a garden and play some games as best we could, but surgery and treatments were a constant presence in our minds.

Round Three

Brain surgery was scheduled for the following Wednesday. The doctors wanted to harvest a tumor that was near the surface and verify that the cancer had spread. Some doctors on the treatment team were of the opinion that they had cured the cancer previously and that this was a new cancer. By harvesting a tumor, they would know for sure. The test results revealed that the cancer was the same cancer at the DNA level, so more chemo and radiation would be the treatment option of choice. Sheryl was already taking an oral chemo pill four times a day. Now a daily dose of radiation would be delivered to her brain stem as a part of the cure. We quickly fell into a daily routine that consisted of getting my son to daycare and then driving my wife to radiation before returning home to work on a few chores before getting our son at the end of the day. Running errands meant having someone come over to the house and sit with Sheryl. The pressure on her brain stem which was causing the dizziness reduced her motor skills to that of a one-year-old. She would need constant supervision.

One day after we'd returned from radiation, I was cleaning up some dishes in the kitchen. I noticed that the knob to turn on the water at the kitchen sink was loose. I knew I should shut the water off at the street just to play it safe. I didn't need a disaster right now, but I reasoned to myself that I was putting it back together so it wouldn't blow apart. I tried to gently secure the knob into place when everything came apart. It took me a moment to recover my senses after a jet of water began flowing past my head towards the ceiling. In a vain attempt to avoid disaster, I clamped my hands over the flow of water and tried to redirect the flow into the sink and down the drain. I also began yelling for my wife to help me. The radiation made her very tired so that when we got home, she would make it to her favorite napping place, the couch. I can usually make myself heard just by raising my voice, but I really had to work at getting her to wake up.

"What are you yelling about?" I heard from the other room.

"Get in here quick! I need your help shutting the water off!"

"Ah, hello. I can't really walk in there. I have this dizzy problem from cancer." In my mind's eye I could see her eyes roll to the very back of her head and probably rested up against the tumor causing the dizziness.

"If ya can't walk, you're gonna have to crawl, but I need you in here NOW!"

I don't know how long it actually took for her to crawl into the kitchen. The couch was only about twenty feet away, but for a person trying to hold back a water main break, it seemed like forever. Because of how I was standing I couldn't see her enter the kitchen. I only felt her presence. Well actually, I felt her trying to pull my legs out of the way so she could get under the sink that I was standing at. I wound up with my legs spread as wide as I could get them spread, and then my wife tried to crawl through them to get under the sink. As she was getting under the sink, she moved from side to side which made me move from side to side too, and whenever I moved, water shot out at odd angles getting us both soaking wet. At one point the jet of water shot into my chest and angled off of me and under the sink hitting her in the middle of the shoulder blades and up to her head. She let out a shriek about how cold the water was and told me to "quit getting her wet!" Like I had a choice in the matter. Truth be told, it probably was only a few seconds or maybe a minute total elapsed time, but to me it seemed like it took hours to get the water shut off at the wall. Because of the angle of the cabinets, the water valves were about four feet under the counter. So, getting my soaking wet wife out from under the sink took a bit of effort. By the time I got her out, we were both laughing, and the water had traveled throughout the majority of the house. It was just another curve ball life threw at us. That water valve could have broken many times before, but it chose that day to come apart, and we had a good laugh before I got dry clothes for us and began mopping up all the water.

The Stress

As a teacher I have some responsibilities that are difficult to avoid. The end of school is one of those responsibilities. I needed to return to work for the last four days of school and close up my grade book and pack up some things in my room. On one of those very stressful days, I entered my class and did my usual thing. I put my lunch in my mini fridge, turned on my computer, and checked to be sure I had the date correct on the white board. As I put my room keys in my pocket, I did what I always do, check to see that my wallet and phone were also in my pocket. I found the phone but couldn't find my wallet. I checked and rechecked my pockets. Checked my coat. Checked the truck. Nothing! I couldn't find it anywhere. I called home and asked my wife's aunt who was sitting with her that day to check my dresser. It wasn't there either. I hadn't left it at home. I knew I had lost it. Immediately I called the bank and canceled my cards. I didn't want whoever got my wallet to drain my bank account, too. I grumbled the rest of the day. When I got home, I changed out of my work clothes and was emptying my pockets. Out came the keys. Out came my phone. Without even thinking about it I reached into my pocket and pulled out my wallet. When I tossed it on the bed, I realized it had been in my pocket all day. I was totally stressed to the point that I was missing things that should have been obvious. I had so many things to do that I was getting less than three hours of sleep a night and keeping myself going with coffee.

The Care Center

Because of the radiation and chemo that Sheryl was enduring, she became very weak. So weak in fact that she couldn't lift her head off the pillow. When my son was born, he could raise his head and look around the room the moment he entered this world. My wife didn't have that kind of strength. The cure was going to kill her long before the disease had a chance to. So, she was hospitalized for a few days to get her system evened out and was then transferred to a care facility.

A case worker entered the hospital room and handed me a list of nursing homes. She was set to be discharged in just a few hours, and I was pressed for a location on where she should continue her care. I made a couple of calls and blindly made my uninformed choice.

On the second day of her stay at the care facility, Sheryl realized she had been transferred from the hospital and really didn't like where she was. She asked me if I would get her out of the nursing home and take her to our home. The hardest conversation I've ever had was when I told her she had to stay at the care home. She was so weak that it took two people to move her. She couldn't raise her head off the pillow let alone get herself bathed or fed or dressed. I was completely unable to care for her at this point due to her weakened state, and it didn't help that the medications she had been taking caused massive weight gain. So, in the course of five weeks, her weight had doubled. Even if she had all of her strength, it would have been difficult for her to get around. The thought of an emergency situation evolved in my mind and how I would be able to get her out of bed and out of the house without help from others. I was forced to leave her in the care facility for a couple of months, the hardest decision I had to make during this time. I made it my daily practice to get to her room as early as I could each morning and share some breakfast with her before I tackled my responsibilities and chores. Sheryl devoted herself to physical therapy and making improvements to her strength. She was determined to beat cancer. I also made sure that Tucker got to visit her every day, but every evening it was a difficult struggle to leave her in the care of others.

The place I decided on was directly across the street from my brother's house. This made it easy for the family to visit Sheryl. My sister-in-law would make regular trips across the street to spend evenings with Sheryl, and they'd watch TV together and talk. Precious moments that were special to share. As she regained her strength, my brother's house was also the location of family gatherings. I'd commandeer a wheelchair and help her get out of bed and "out on a pass." Each Sunday afternoon for about a month we would all gather and have a small snack or a piece of pie and catch up on things. Nothing important, just time together. Those would be the last times our whole family would be able to gather. They were informal and unscripted and because of Sheryl's lagging strength, short—usually an hour or less—but in looking back, they became very important. It was good to have Sheryl staying close to family while she was in the care home. Even now, many years later, whenever we visit my brother's house and get out of the truck, my son will pause and look at the place where his mom was housed while she regained her strength. It's only a passing moment, but it's a somber moment. The only comment he'll make is, "I hate that place." I make sure he knows that I feel the same way.

At Home

What was supposed to take a year or more would take only five months. Sheryl was on a downward slide, and there was nothing we could do to stop it from happening. So, we made her as comfortable as we could. Hospice was the new treatment plan. Some friends asked if they could set up a bedroom for her, and I was pleased to have the help. This included repainting the room in her favorite color, pink and hanging some pretty, feminine, girly things (Sheryl lived with two guys. If it wasn't car related, it was a challenge to get it in the house). Included were some medical things like a hospital bed and some chairs for visitors to sit in while they talked with Sheryl. It was a haven for her, a peaceful place where she could get out of the main room of the house and out of our bedroom where I might be doing something like folding clothes. It was her room. It was in this room that she informed me that I was going to have to learn how to cook.

You need to know that the last time I'd tried to cook anything beyond a pizza, I started a fire on the stove top that would have gotten into the vent had I not used a fire extinguisher to put it out. At the time, I couldn't keep track of my wallet or a hundred other things, and now I'm supposed to learn a new skill? But she was right. I needed to know how to cook. We couldn't just live off of pizza. A couple of days later Sheryl was sitting on the couch— yes, the very place she'd crawled from to help shut off the water—and my son asked for some Mac 'n Cheese.

"You're gonna have to learn some time, it might as well be now." I had been married for twenty-four years, and I knew that tone in her voice. I wasn't getting out of this.

"Okay, I'll give it a shot." I went to the garage, retrieved a fire extinguisher, and placed it near the stove. "Here goes." I said a prayer in hopes the house wouldn't burn to the ground.

"First get out the big saucepan, the one I make spaghetti sauce in, and fill it up about two-thirds with water and get it to a good boil on the stove. Let me know when you have big bubbles rolling in the pan." On and on it went. Step by step, I learned how to cook Mac 'n Cheese. It was a skill I would need and another level of stress. My world was changing and the paradigm shifting.

Many things happened the last few weeks of Sheryl's life. People came by each day to visit. People from our Sunday school group at church were a constant presence in our home. Some of them would stay the night sleeping on the floor next to the hospital bed and give me a break from caring for Sheryl. We had a travel trailer at the time, and I took to sleeping in it at night. The front door of my house was never locked. There was always someone visiting or checking in or dropping off food. In fact, we had so many visitors that Tucker was transitioned to my parents' house at night so he would be able to get some sleep. They would get him to daycare in the mornings. Yet another load I didn't need to carry for a few weeks.

Many people came by just to stop in and say hello. One person carried their diet Pepsi with them as they visited. Sheryl needed something to drink, so she called out to me to get her something. The visitor apologized and said, "Oh I'm sorry if I'd thought about it, I could have brought you a diet Pepsi, too." Without batting an eyelid, Sheryl responded, "Oh I don't drink diet soda. I hear it causes cancer." (crickets could be heard in the background) "Well, I guess we can see how well that worked out, huh." The visitor didn't know how to respond, but Sheryl had a good laugh from it.

My goal was to make Sheryl comfortable and see her off with dignity and grace. I think I achieved my goals. Many people came and went. I did a load of dishes. People came and went. I folded a load of clothes. People came and went. I heated some food for dinner. Sheryl took a nap, I played a game with my son, and each day Sheryl slipped a little farther away.

On her last Sunday of life, she had a difficult night sleeping. She was wrestling in her mind with leaving Tucker. She finally decided that today was the day to tell him she was going to die. It was a sweet conversation between a dying mother and her young son. A few minutes later Sheryl turned to me and stated simply, "I've lived out my calendar. I don't have any more plans. I think I can die now." That was at 8 o'clock in the morning. By dinner time she was beginning to have difficulty holding a conversation. By Monday evening confusion was such a constant that when her phone rang, she tried to answer the TV remote. By Tuesday, her sentences were reduced to a few words. Conversation became difficult and confusing. Her will to live had kept her going, kept her mentally involved in life. Once she gave up, it was only a matter of a hours before she passed.

My house had seen a constant stream of people both night and day for almost a month, but as things worked out that Tuesday night, it was just Sheryl and I. Dinner arrived early, and I ate it while her last visitor tried to carry on a short conversation with her. Then the hospice nurse came by for a checkup. Sheryl was getting restless and having difficulty settling in for the evening, so the nurse had me give her some meds to help her relax. It was significant to me because Sheryl had to have help sitting up. She couldn't take the meds lying on her back, and she needed help staying upright to swallow the meds with some water. As the meds took effect, she was restless, and I could tell she was wrestling with something in her mind. About midnight she settled into a deep sleep. Knowing the end was near kept me awake all night. I couldn't relax and get any rest, so I was still wide awake at 4 AM when she sat straight upright in bed, looked past me, and said very matter-of-factly, "I need to go." She laid back down and fell back to sleep. I think that was the point her spirit departed. Her body was still present and functioning, but she wasn't responding to any stimulation. And why would she? She wasn't around, she'd left. About 6 AM I began to call people and let them know we had reached the last few hours of her life. My house almost immediately, once again, filled with people. Family members, and friends, people from our church group and from her work, carloads of people would show up and join the growing crowd. I was ready to get breakfast. I hadn't had but half a meal from the night before, had been up all night and was hungry.

"Anyone want to go to go out for breakfast with me?" I asked the group. My pastor calmly instructed me to stay at home and hang loose. I wasn't allowed to leave. Just before 11 AM, Sheryl passed away in her hospital bed, in her hospice room painted pink, and decorated with pretty, girly things. She was surrounded by family and friends.

Tucker was still at school. His grandparents had made sure he attended that day. We got him dismissed early. As he walked up the driveway, he became aware of the large number of people present. Ten people were standing in my front yard because there wasn't a seat available for them to sit on inside. Fear began to wash over his face. I knelt down to talk with him face-to-face. I wanted to be at his level. He drew up close to me and peered around my shoulder, fear beginning to be replaced with wonder. I told him that Mamma had gone to heaven like they had talked about and took him by the hand as we entered the house to say our goodbyes. Soon Tucker would get to go with Gram and Pops. He would spend the rest of the day and night with them while I stayed home. There was a delay in the mortuary getting the body, so it was late afternoon before Sheryl left, and then shortly after that, all the family that had hung around began to leave, too. A good friend of mine, Steve, had taken my phone soon after I had made a couple of calls letting family and work know what had happened. He screened my calls for the rest of the day and managed the crowd. This was huge. It allowed me space to grieve and work things thorough in my mind. At 7 o'clock that evening I was left alone. I went to the trailer for the night. I had been on the go for exactly thirty-six hours. Exhaustion doesn't even begin to describe my state. I wasn't making any decisions, just functioning. It didn't take long to fall asleep, but I clearly remember thinking to myself, now maybe things would return to normal.

The next day I got myself moving. I was barred from driving or using my phone, so a friend had volunteered to drive me around and help me get my life back on track. I began the process of getting a body cremated, planning a memorial service, setting in motion a graveside service and all the other thousands of decisions I needed to make. Work was gracious and let me have an additional three weeks off. For that I was eternally grateful.

Memorial Rant

I hate memorial services. Not so much because we are bidding our dearly departed goodbye. Saying goodbye is sad, so leave me alone and let me remember them in peace. The part I hate is when people feel like they need to say something. Maybe it's because I speak in front of groups daily or because I've played lots of music on stage in bands and orchestras, but most people who speak at a funeral shouldn't. Nobody cares about the one funny birthday card. Nobody wants to hear you sniffle into the microphone that you just pointed at the speakers causing the high-pitched squeal from the sound system. Thanks to you, baby dolphins halfway around the globe had a moment of pain as the feedback interfered with their sonar. Nobody wants to hear the song you wrote on the way to the funeral. These things should all be kept to yourself. If you're in charge of planning a memorial service, plan it out. Don't let the attendees sit until someone feels uncomfortable with the silence, so they get up and share yet another unremarkable tidbit about this loved one. We don't need to hear the same story five times from five different people. Do we need organ music? Unless that person was an organist, probably not. If they were a musician, maybe we should hear some of the music they played instead.

All these thoughts were swirling around my brain as I contemplated what to do for a memorial service. So, step one, contact current and past musicians that Sheryl and I had played with and put an impromptu band together and have them play some pieces that Sheryl loved. Step two, gather letters from loved ones and family members, friends and coworkers. These can be edited and read by one or two people as a part of the service. By editing the contents, you don't have things repeated. Each letter is a fresh memory. Step three, gather pictures to be used in a memorial slide show and get someone trustworthy to complete that project. So, I had my work cut out for me. Many decisions to be made. The three weeks flew by. Every day was filled with things needing to be accomplished as quickly as possible. In the end, I had put together a concise, one-hour service that had many memories read by two different people, and a rock band that would play while people came in and could double as a bluegrass band for some gospel hymns that Sheryl loved to sing. A memorial slide show was played, and the preacher was able to deliver the message he felt needed to be shared.

The day was a full day. Usually, the church we attend would host the family for a meal after the service, but because the service was being held on a Saturday, we had to be out of the church as soon after 2PM as possible so that Sunday preparations could be made. Because there were many family members from out of town who had attended the graveside service the day before, I requested that we have brunch instead. That worked well for everyone. The service started at 1PM, but Tucker and I arrived by about 10AM to answer any questions and help get things ready. When we entered the hall where brunch was being served, I was surprised and a little overcome because all of the people who were a part of the kitchen crew had used pink hair spray and were sporting pink hair, reminiscent of the pink mohawk I'd given Sheryl three years before. After our meal together and time visiting with family, Tucker and I made our way to a Sunday school classroom where we changed into our suits. Sheryl made me promise that I'd wear a suit to her funeral. She knew how much I hated dressing up, so she made me promise, and I kept my promise. Tucker and I sported pink canvas tennis shoes. Pink was the color of choice that day. After the service, I stood in the lobby of the church for over an hour greeting people who had come to pay their last respects. Many tears were shed along with some smiles and many hugs. In fact, I had to have the suit cleaned because of all the makeup that managed to get on the lapel of the coat.

By now I was emotionally wrung out. I could hardly function as I made my way back to the classroom and got changed back into my casual clothes. My friend had been a huge help all day and had been a comforting presence for hours. He was in a hurry to get on his way, but I stopped him and made sure he understood how thankful I was for all his help. He started to get into his car, but he stood up and turned to me and stated very clearly, "You can expect that all the people who have been supporting you these last few months will drift away, and you'll find that your support network pretty much doesn't exist."

"Ok," I said, "I'll try to be prepared for it to happen."

Time with Sheryl before Tucker was born.

On a hike at a nearby scenic area.

Our first family photo.

Fun filled family time at a park.

My favorite picture from this period of our lives. The final battle with cancer will begin in just a couple of months. Sheryl is post treatment and we have just returned home from a fun filled family outing.

Sheryl just a few months before Tucker was born.

A very unimpressed toddler learning about cameras.

Mom and son on a train ride at a nearby zoo.

Regaining strength after chemo. Some days were easier than others, so we made sure to bring the wagon along.

Relaxing in the front yard. The idea of a cancer battle hasn't crossed our minds. Tucker who was not yet two took this photo.

The pink mohawk that everyone remembers.

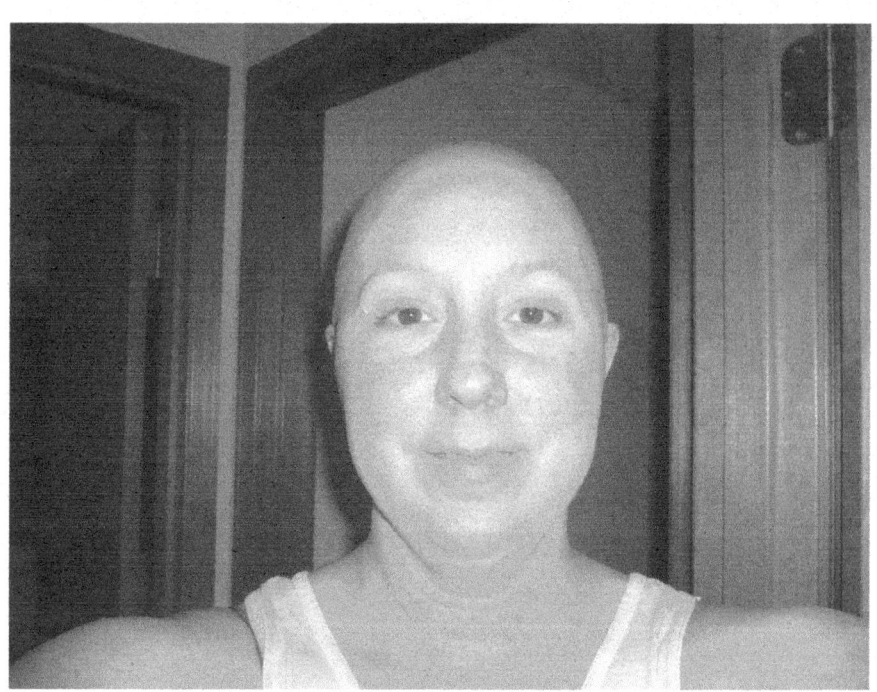

Determined to beat the disease and Fight Like A Girl (FLAG)!!!!! But she mostly did it without any hair.

Fun times with Mom and Son. Enjoying a second chance at life after our initial cancer fight.

A fun time at the Oregon Coast on a good day during the radiation period of treatment.

A selfie onboard an innertube in the snowy mountains of Oregon on our last family outing. Two weeks later Sheryl would begin to feel the effect of the tumors pressing on her brain stem.

Our last family photo. The results of the infamous trip to the photo studio.

All By Myself

Moving on

WE HELD THE MEMORIAL SERVICE on a Saturday. After the service, Tucker and I made our get away to the Oregon Coast for one night. By Monday we were back at school. He was attending kindergarten for half days and then childcare for the afternoons. It was a perfect place for Tucker to begin to find some rhythm in his young life. I had one day to get up to speed at my school. Where were classes in the pacing of the curriculum? What print needed to be ordered? What was going to be my first assignment of the year? So many questions that needed answers, and I couldn't think straight. I reasoned it was just because I was tired. All I needed was some rest, but at night I couldn't sleep. I could fall asleep on the couch at 6 o'clock and sleep for hours. Because of this I needed to keep moving when I got home from work. No sitting down or I was done, and Tucker wasn't getting fed, but when 11 o'clock or midnight came around I couldn't relax and fall asleep. Then chores would begin to press into my train of thought. Many nights I was still awake after 2:30 AM. The alarm always goes off at 5:30 so I can be at my desk in the school by 7AM. I wasn't getting any sleep. Without sleep I couldn't function. So, I began drinking more coffee. The first year after Sheryl died, I could easily consume 12-15 shots of espresso throughout the course of a day. Coffee became my crutch.

In the months that followed Sheryl's passing, I struggled to get through each day. I felt like I had fourteen bowling pins that I needed to keep in the air at all times. I still felt like I was carrying a heavy burden, a lead blanket that slowed my every move, and I couldn't keep up. There was always something to do and never enough time to do things right. Getting groceries became one of my first challenges to overcome. Sheryl was a milk drinker, and between her and Tucker, they could down more than two gallons in a week's time. A trip to the big box bargain store always meant visiting the diary room and getting two gallons of milk. It would last a few days and I'd have to get more from the store. Because I don't drink milk it was up to Tucker to drink all the milk. Of course, that didn't happen. So, I was pouring gallons of sour milk down the drain each week. We had plenty of some things and none of the other. In my confused state, I purchased a big container of cotton swabs, forgot I had them, and the next time I went to the store purchased another big container of cotton swabs. I now had a stockpile of cotton swabs that I'm still trying to get rid of many years later. I needed to get organized, but the fog I was operating in was keeping me from organizing my thoughts let alone my house or cupboards. I was caught up in the idea that certain chores needed to be done at specific times during the day. Dishes should be done immediately after we eat, or so I thought, but that meant that I wasn't spending time with my son in the evenings. So, I switched the order of evening activities. Dishes got cleaned after he went to bed. This allowed me to get dinner ready while he played with toys, and then we'd spend some time together after dinner.

Getting groceries was a skill that I thought I had mastered, but now I had to get groceries that I wasn't sure I'd need and was missing getting some things I would need and was trying to corral a four-year-old at the same time. Things needed to change. The first thing I did was get Tucker involved. He became my cart operator. This served three purposes: one. It kept him occupied and in one place. I didn't have to worry about losing him in a store. 2. It freed me up to get food off the shelves and use a grocery list. 3. People moved out of the way of the junior operator (nobody wanted to get run over), which allowed me to move quickly and unobstructed down the aisles meaning little opportunity for my now five-year-old to get bored and wander off.

Sheryl had developed the skill of cooking from scratch and using foods she cooked for more than one meal. So, a roast would be accompanied by potatoes. The roast would then be used later in the week for fajitas or meat pies or any other dish that could use roast meat. The potatoes could be used for breakfast or mashed. I didn't have the skill to do that, so I made the switch to cooking out of a box. Pasta and rice were easy to make. I could cook ground beef in a skillet and a bag of frozen veggies was easy to heat up. That being said, I still struggled. There are a couple of saucepans that bear the scars of my trying to heat up food. Not everything was tasty, but it was sustenance. Now I had to figure out how to get it tasting good. I began to make a list of meals I could make and the food we'd need for each meal. This helped control the amount of food that came into the house and limited what was thrown out from spoilage.

During this time, I was still getting help for my evening meals. While I was away from work, my church kept me supplied with meals. Once I returned to work, many of my coworkers began to help out, too. They'd wanted to help for many months, but I wasn't in contact, so they didn't know when or how to get me food. As it worked out, I was given meals for a couple of months after I returned to work. This helped me get back into the "normal" routine and eased my demand for groceries, but I found myself with seemingly inexhaustible supplies of some things.

Routine?

Life isn't all about groceries, but it is a perfect example of how my life was changing. The normal I expected to return to never materialized. As I drove away from Sheryl's memorial service I was expecting, hoping, praying for a return to the old routine. There is comfort in routine. I had been used to the same basic routine for more than two decades. Now everything was changing. My memories of that first year are bleak memories. A heaviness hangs over all of it. Just organizing a trip to the grocery store took all my mental acuity and physical endurance. Slogging through life was taking all of my energy and I was failing at some tasks. Amongst the confusion one instance stands out. My son would be going on a field trip with school. I was supposed to get him a sack lunch only I never did. I either never saw an email or I had misplaced the email and forgotten about the trip. I sent my son to school expecting the lunch program to take care of his meal. Because I forgot, someone out of the goodness of their heart had to get him something to eat. On this occasion it meant a trip to Subway for a sandwich. My mind wasn't processing the information like it needed to.

A part of this is the grief process. I was told and have since learned from experience that the first year is the worst. Once you clear that hurdle, it gets better. I'd like to say that this period in my life was a time of personal growth and improvement, but romantic comedies aren't reality. I didn't have time to improve. I barely had the time and skills to keep from failing completely.

Camper Life

"Do not make any major life altering decisions for at least a year," people say. I kept to that advice except for one thing: I traded in my travel trailer for a camper that fit neatly into the back of my pickup. My trailer was twenty-seven feet long which meant that when it was being towed my overall length was close to fifty feet. By switching to a camper, I reduced my length to twenty-eight feet. It was much nimbler and fit in more places. I was also able to back up without the need for assistance from an adult. This was important. If I made a wrong turn and needed to back up onto a busy road or turn around in a parking lot, I would need adult assistance. Now, if I needed to back up into a camping spot, I was able to perform the task on my own without putting any other vehicles or buildings in jeopardy.

As the years have progressed, my son and I have spent many weeks traveling around the western United States. We are both on school calendars, so we are free for ten weeks each summer. We've taken advantage of this free time. It is common for us to be gone for 6-8 weeks at a time. If you start in Texas and begin traveling north through Oklahoma and the grasslands, eventually you will make your way to North Dakota. That line of states is how far east we traveled as we meandered through our summer vacations. This also meant that I had hours to spend behind the wheel processing and thinking and dealing with life. I worked out many problems, concerns, and hurts over the thousands of miles we traveled. Switching from a trailer to a camper was the best thing I did that first year.

As much fun as we've had with the camper, there is also one day that sticks in my mind and is representative of the pain I was dealing with at the time. It was a Saturday, and Tucker was spending the day with a friend. I was at home grading papers and working on the chores necessary to keep my house functioning. I kept going to the window looking for Sheryl. When was she going to be home? What was delaying her? Did the car break down or did she have an accident? Those questions would wash through my mind as I looked expectantly out the front window of my home. And then I'd remember that she wasn't coming home. I wouldn't be able to show her the new camper. I wouldn't be able to share any camper experience with her. The loneliness and pain would again try to consume me from the inside. Heartburn, probably from all the coffee, would rise in my throat, and I would walk away from the window with tears welling in my eyes. This happened all afternoon, too many times to count. Steps that I had made to move forward and put my past behind me actually entrapped me and caused me additional pain. This was my new normal.

Church

I wasn't able to attend church while Sheryl was sick. Once she passed away, I was eager to return to my fellowship and begin refreshing my soul. That first Sunday back, I quietly made my way to a pew with about five minutes to go before the service started. I chose a seat in a pew that was partially empty with couples seated in the pews either in front of me or behind me. I quickly scanned the informational hand out and tried to see what I'd been missing. After a couple of minutes, I looked up to realize that those who had been sitting near me had all moved. No one was within two rows of me, and the people who had been sitting at the other end of the pew had also moved. I had been sitting near people and now was in the middle of a bubble and no one was any closer to me than fifteen feet. Talk about making someone feel unwelcome. Since this time, I have talked with a friend whose husband died from cancer about the same time that Sheryl died. She experienced the same thing at her church. No one would sit near her. We now sit with each other when we attend church just so we have someone to sit with; otherwise, there is no guarantee that we won't be sitting all alone.

At the same time I realized I was sitting all by myself, the music started. I love music. I've played in bands both in church and out of church. I've played in concert bands and orchestras. The music portion of a church service is my favorite. It's so much more enjoyable than when the pastor gets up front and talks. What I hadn't realized was that for the 24 years that I'd been married plus the two years that we'd dated, I had always listened for the part that my wife was singing so I could sing the second harmony part. I was standing all by myself, and I couldn't hear the other harmony being sung, so I didn't know what part to sing. I felt utterly and completely alone. Even God didn't want to sit with me.

By now friends who had been helping me with Sheryl had quit calling me. There was nothing for them to be updated about. My phone had grown quiet, but I still held out hope that church would be refreshing. Instead, church became a time where I felt like God wasn't there at all. When the music started, it was like God went and sat with someone else. A couple of times someone within the church leadership would ask me how I was doing. I would tell them I was struggling under the new norm.

"Well go to church, that's the best place to be," was the usual response. Church was the last place I wanted to be. It was the place I felt the most alone.

I wanted my son to grow up with a grounding in church life, but that meant that I needed to be at church for both hours. And that I had to attend the adult Sunday school class. I had gone with Sheryl, so this wasn't a foreign activity to me. The next Sunday I decided I'd take in both hours at church. I sat amongst people who had prayed for us and helped me care for Sheryl and I think generally cared for me, people I considered my friends. I should have been comforted, but every time the door would open, I would look up expecting to see my wife come through the door. By the end of the hour, I couldn't get out of the room fast enough. Because it had been six months since I'd been to church, people wanted to get caught up and see how things were going. I needed to escape. There wasn't enough air in the room for me to be able to breath. I honestly tried many times to go back, but every time I did, I had the same experience. I kept looking for my wife. I always left with an empty feeling in my soul and a few minutes later I'd have to go and sit by myself and wonder what had happened to God.

On this first day back to church a very nice lady who was an acquaintance and had been through some very difficult times came up to me and gave me a big hug. She told me that "camping in the Psalms" had been a blessing for her and she thought if I did the same, I would benefit from it. I made sure I followed her advice, and I did find solace within those scriptures. Psalm twenty-three paints a pretty good picture of what I'd been through the last few years. I had enjoyed the green pasture life described in the first couple of verses. Church had been enjoyable for me, and I had grown and strengthened my faith. I had experienced the "valley of the shadow of death" verses, too, as I helped my wife in her last few months, but that's where the similarities ended. In my mind, I pictured God leading me through that valley, and then, instead of the celebration I was led into the wilderness and left on my own. Over the next few months, I worked my way into the bass player slot on the worship band. The other bass player was having health issues and couldn't play very often. So within a few weeks of Sheri's passing, I was the bass player. This was a good fit for me. I had to be in church for both services. This meant that my son would be in Sunday school class for both hours and get the spiritual grounding I wanted him to have. During the music time, I was on stage and unable to be in the pew listening for my wife's voice. If I was feeling extra sensitive about being asked how things were going, I could always hide out backstage. I had grown tired of people whom I didn't know coming up to me and asking how I was doing, only for them to reply with an empty platitude. So, I began to sequester myself backstage.

Because I was on stage and in the band, I was expected to dress up more than the average person in our church. This meant a dress shirt and usually a tie. Jeans and a polo just weren't gonna cut it for this gig. We were also instructed to wear black as a basic color choice. It's a musician thing. Think of your favorite orchestra. They all wear black. Same with rockers. So being clad all in black wasn't something foreign to me, but the idea of musicians wearing black was lost on one particular church lady. It didn't take but a few weeks for her to approach me and inform me that I needed to quit mourning for my wife. She had decided that it was time for me to quit wearing all black and move on. My period of mourning should be over and I needed to quit living in the past by dragging it out. Bless her heart.

Most people don't like being in front of big crowds, and sometimes I get asked how I can be on stage and play like I do. The simple truth is that being on stage is safe. Because you're in front of many people, the "church ladies" won't approach you. You're left alone. I found comfort in being on stage.

Coffee? Anyone?

This was an interesting time for me. My old friends were leaving me alone and not calling me or talking to me. I was lonely because I had no contact with anyone. If I called anyone and asked if we could get together for a cup of coffee, they were always pretty busy and would get back to me after they checked their schedule, but when they'd see me at church, they always wanted to help me out any way they could. All I needed to do was just ask. It took a couple of months, but I got the message loud and clear. My support had ended. At the same time, I was making friends in the church band. These people understood what I was going though. The leader's wife had lost her mother to cancer. He understood when I was having a bad day. His brother was in the band and was on his second marriage. The guitar player was also on his second marriage and had been a single dad of two girls. He became a source of counseling and problem solving as I found my way through each week. He was also grounded in rock music. Rehearsal times usually included a few chords from any one of the many bands from the 80s. Some nights it was "Name That Tune" or name that artist who sang this tune. We had many good laughs together. When I spoke of my trials, they would each nod and say, "Oh yea I remember those days." Then the advice would follow. "I had the same problem. Here's what I did...." I wasn't being served empty platitudes but real life answers to my needs and hurts. The big room in a church where everybody meets is sometimes called a sanctuary. For me, the band became my sanctuary.

A small part of this support came in the form of our weekly trip for fast food breakfast. After the music portion had ended in the first service, we'd jump in someone's car and grab breakfast. Sometimes this was a serious trip and other times we laughed. Even though it was just a quick trip, it was a connection for me to what life used to be like: time with friends just going out.

Sheryl and I had some casual friends that we would get together with occasionally. This was a group of five couples who were all interconnected in some way either because we knew them through church or we worked with them. In the previous couple of years, we had celebrated the Super Bowl with a party. We had lots of food and hearty laughs. I was so looking forward to the Super Bowl party this year and was anticipating the invite. In the course of events surrounding Sheryl's memorial service, my son was in control of my phone for limited periods of time. This meant that my phone got dropped more than once and the glass cracked badly. I couldn't just buy another phone because they're expensive. I began to use Sheryl's. I was paying for it each month and Sheryl wasn't using it. I carried two phones with me everywhere I went just in case someone called or texted me and then used Sheryl's phone if

I needed to contact someone else. It was a smooth system. Nobody had called me in months. A couple of times I called from one phone to the other just to be sure they both still worked. So, it took a couple of messages to come into Sheryl's phone before I realized I was getting some texts. As I opened up the phone, I was excited cause someone cared enough to spend the time to see how I was doing. I read,

"This is the official invite to the Super Bowl party. Yes, we are having it. Be sure to bring your favorite snack food and we'll provide the drinks. I hope you all can come, but please nobody tell Todd about the party. I really don't want to see them. Don't get me wrong, I loved Sheryl but am so sorry she died because now Tucker will be raised only by his dad and that's gonna ruin Tucker. He really needed Sheryl as his mom to make him a better person."

The texts kept coming in one after another.

"We will be at the party. And I agree, life was better when Sheryl was here.

"Count us in. We'll be there. Knowing I don't have to see Todd will make it a better day."

Each text detailed how terrible a person I was and how much I was loathed. It took me a while to figure out that Sheryl's phone was being included in a previous group chat. Only Sheryl's name was probably hidden, and they didn't know my phone was broken. I wasn't spying on the group, I was using a phone I was paying for. They had been careless about who was included in this chain of texts, but those people I thought were my friends weren't really who I thought they were. I had been in contact off and on with the "camping in the Psalms" lady. I texted her and asked if she was my friend. Her response told me everything I needed to know. She really wanted to keep her distance from me.

She and everyone else. I was shaken and I was hurt. Now more than ever I needed a friend. Someone who would call me just to see if I was alive, and all but one of the people that I had considered to be friends had basically walked away from our relationship.

For a few weeks I was deeply hurt. Only after I heard about the events of the day did I realize I had been spared many troubles. One of the guys in our group helped manage the national television broadcast signals and said he had to work that day and couldn't make the party. One of the ladies managed a makeup counter at a large department store. She wouldn't be able to make it either, but part way through the activities of the day someone was on their phone and realized that TV guy and makeup lady were both at a nearby motel. The entire party managed to catch the couple exiting the motel room together. I was hated by the ladies in the group, but that hatred for me spared me from the ensuing drama.

Totally Alone

The realization of being totally alone hit me a few weeks later as I was driving through town. My son was spending the night at his grandparents' house, and I was out in the late evening running errands. A car veered into my lane and almost hit my truck. I thought about the consequences. My truck would have been ruined, and I could have been lying in a ditch for hours before anyone came looking for me. In fact, nobody would need to know where I was or what I was doing until the next morning when I didn't show up for work. During the 24 years I was married, I always checked in with Sheryl. She always knew where I was and who I was with. If I were at a band practice, I would call her before I left the rehearsal. That way she would know practice had ended and I was on the road. If I were coaching a game, before I left the parking lot, I would send her a text: headed home. If I didn't arrive home by a reasonable time, she needed to come and find me. I was either broken down or in an accident. I no longer had that covering. I had no one to check in with. If I had needed some emergency help, could I have called on any one of the people I knew? Maybe, but I think the response would have been hit or miss. Usually once every week or ten days, one of my parents would call to see if I was still alive, but in the months since the memorial service no one else cared enough to call or text just to check on me. I felt like I'd been left alone.

In my mind I see each of us as a player on a team in a sports stadium. The people on our team and in the stands are all friends and acquaintances. People who are friends are supposed to encourage you and spend time with you and together we cheer each other on. In my stadium everyone was missing. The stadium was empty. Even the grounds crew was missing.

I made a mental adjustment. I decided to leave my current stadium and "play" in a different, smaller stadium. I quit seeking out people. I quit looking at my phone hoping someone would take me up on my offer for coffee. I quit expecting anyone to care about me or my son. From here on it was just he and I. We would get through it together. Once I made that determination, my life improved. I no longer anticipated a call from anyone. Many days would pass, and I wouldn't even turn on either phone. They would sit powered off. Because I wasn't anticipating anyone getting in touch, the feelings of loneliness left. I was alone but not lonely. My life improved just a little.

Things were different now. People who I thought were friends avoided me. One instance stands out in my mind. I was walking down a hallway at church and my path took me by a "friend." I greeted them by name. "Hey so-and-so, how ya doing?" This person wouldn't make eye contact or acknowledge my presence. Instead, this person turned their head so they were facing away from me and looked very intently at a blank wall and just kept on walking. Another time, I tried to ask a different "friend" if her daughter and Tucker could have a playdate. We were standing in the front lobby at church. She informed me that she wouldn't talk to me because her husband wasn't around to supervise the conversation. I needed to be aware that because I was single and she was married, things were different now. What? You can't be serious, I thought. Before I could find the words to respond, she turned and walked away. I was just asking a question. My son and her daughter were friends, and he really wanted the play time. I hadn't asked her anything inappropriate. We were apparently stuck in puritan New England. This was crazy. I was hurt that people would ignore me or avoid me. These had been the very people who were telling me they were praying for me and that they cared. I retreated further into myself and stayed mostly backstage at the church.

Learning To Cook

Meanwhile, I was still trying to learn how to cook. One evening, I was struggling to get my dinner prepared. My son wanted Mac 'n Cheese again, so along with my meal, I also had that on the stove. It didn't take me long to figure out that my dinner wasn't going to be edible. It was supposed to be a casserole but had the consistency of thin soup. Maybe I could order a pizza again. At this point in my life, I absolutely hated Mac 'n Cheese. Chile Mac was a main staple while I was in the Army. This is nasty. It's government chili with government macaroni and topped with government cheese. It has the consistency of wet cement and tastes like cardboard. YUK! Thirty years later, I'm still emotionally scarred, but that was all that I was going to have access to on this particularly stormy night. If I was going to eat it, I had to make it tasty. I reached for other ingredients not included in the box. Sour Cream, a scoop of cream cheese and lots of cheddar jack cheese with some garlic powder rounded out what wound up in the pan. When I served it, I included some bacon pieces on top. Everything's better with bacon, I thought. When I sat down to eat what I'd cooked, it wasn't too bad. I realized I wasn't stuck with what was in the box. I could make improvements. For a few months I had worked in a nearby plant making paint. I worked from a recipe. One batch began with 450 gallons of solvent, and I added clay and resin and other chemicals to make a primer. If I could do that, why couldn't I follow a food recipe? I began to experiment. Not everything worked out. Many nights were spent at our favorite burger joint or getting a pizza because I'd burned dinner or it simply wasn't edible. The fact that we didn't get food poisoning or die of starvation is proof that there is a Divine Creator who really cares about us. We lived through that first year. Tucker still loves to tell the story of one night as we were camping, I forgot to put cooking utensils in the camper. I needed to stir my pasta, so I reached for a plastic knife. Let me be clear about one thing I learned that night: plastic knives melt in boiling water. By the time my pasta had cooked my knife was at least an inch and a half shorter than the other knives in the package. The good news was my pasta was very shiny and bright. It almost sparkled. As soon as we got home from our trip, I made sure there were cooking utensils present in the camper.

Music Therapy

Because I was playing in the band at church, I needed to practice new music and get my skills back up. I had packed all my gear away when Tucker was little. He was born during my first year as a teacher, so I didn't have time to play if I'd wanted to. Everything was packed in a closet. Then, just as I was thinking of getting a guitar out, Sheryl got sick, and that consumed all my time, but now I had a regular gig, and I needed to refresh my skills. So, I kept a guitar near the TV. I would get Tucker to bed and complete my chores, and then I would pick up the guitar and spend a few minutes noodling around just exploring chords. Sometimes I'd play a new song I needed to learn or a favorite from the 80s. I quickly figured out that this time spent with my guitar was therapy. If I was down, my song choice usually was a slow, sad song. I learned a song from my childhood about a guy whose wife had died. Bobby Goldsboro and I had something in common, and on the most difficult nights I would play and sing along.

It brought pain. It brought loneliness. Tears would flow as I worked through the chords, but it was a vehicle I needed to grab a hold of the emotional pain and squeeze the life out of it. What I found out about myself was that if I avoided the sadness and loneliness, then it would persist and I couldn't leave it alone. I would return to it over the course of many days, but if I focused on the pain, focused on the loneliness, focused on the cause of my distress, I could leave all of my pain in a heap on the floor of my emotional room. Playing guitar helped me with that process because I could only play the song so many times before it was time to move on to something better.

It was about this time that I visited my favorite burger shack. Now you must know that over the many years that I had been married, we had dined at this establishment thousands of times. I hadn't darkened its door for a couple of years, so as I entered the parking lot, I was anticipating a most excellent meal. My son was enjoying a play date with a friend which included dinner, so I was on my own. I ordered and started down the aisle to my usual seat. Only it was occupied by a young couple. They had the newly-married look about them, too, all warm and glowy and couldn't care less about anyone else in the place. I needed to find a different place to sit. As I made my way around that restaurant, the memories flooded in. We had made it our dinner spot one semester while I was getting my bachelor's degree. I had a late class at Oregon State and was also taking an evening class at the local community college. We had just enough time to grab a burger at the shack. One year I helped my parents flip a house. Lunch time often found us at the shack. That fall, a holiday glass was awarded if you ordered a particular meal. My parents got a set of twelve holiday glasses that year for Christmas. All these memories plus many more overwhelmed me as I choked down my food. I couldn't enjoy my meal. The fries turned to lead in my stomach. I left half my burger and didn't partake of the dessert. I felt sick to my stomach. I had been having a good week. I was feeling positive. I was almost happy at times, and this trip was supposed to be my reward for doing so well. My evening meal turned out to be an emotional sucker punch. Depressed and lonely, I made my way home. I didn't feel good enough to play guitar for many hours. Tucker came home and had gone to bed, and I was feeling bad because I'd hardly said a word to him. I felt like I was back at square one the night of Sheryl's memorial service.

Grief had ambushed me. It happened so fast I needed a replay, and I replayed all my memories from that night. It was near midnight when I reached for my guitar. I needed some therapy. I noodled for a few minutes, and then my fingers began to make the correct chords while I hummed along. Once I got past the event of Sheryl dying, this was the worst night of my life. I had never been so depressed. Not before or since. I wasn't wanting to harm myself or anyone else. I didn't need to be medicated. I just needed to recover from my trip down memory lane. As a result of that trip to my once favorite burger shack, I learned to guard where I went. There are simply some places I no longer go because of the strong memories I have from the time I was married. I haven't been to the shack since that night many years ago. I won't go back either. I don't want to visit the memories. I have learned to guard myself.

As I write these words the musician in me has decided I need to revisit my song of distress, "Honey." I am happy to say that I don't remember all the chords. I haven't needed to play that song in quite a while. As things progressed, I would work past my grief, and my life would begin to even out. Yes, there are still difficult days. We all have them from time to time. And yes, I still play guitar and have one sitting next to my TV because I still need counseling, but these days my songs have a happier subject.

Beginning to Function Again

The first year after my wife passed was by far the most difficult in my life. I had very little sleep and the sleep I got was troubled. I had many stresses that plagued me after I fell asleep, so I wasn't getting any rest. I longed for a few days to unplug and rest and problem-solve. My first opportunity came during spring break that year. My one huge life change was that camper. It was large, so there were separate sleeping areas for both my son and myself. It had a shower and kitchen area. We were self-sufficient, and I could get away, and I made sure I had it stocked with the necessities needed for cooking and sleeping and bathing. No more short plastic knives when I cooked pasta!

This trip was to Astoria, Oregon and all the historic sites in that region. I had so much fun learning local history, but evenings were the most beneficial. After dinner we played board games, and then my son was off to bed by mid evening. That left me a few hours to think and review. I began to identify obstacles that I was placing in my way each day that were holding me back from being successful in my outlook on life and my duties as a parent. I had been having trouble keeping up with the laundry. I had always done the laundry, so I was bothered by it not being done. I would later go out and buy three bins that dirty laundry went into. I didn't wait to sort it out at the end of the week but made a choice to sort laundry every couple of days. When a bin was half full it was time to do a load. I began to plan differently for meals. I wasn't going to always default to a restaurant when I failed to cook dinner. That meant I needed to get extra food and plan options. That meant another layer of planning, but as I thought through my daily activities, I began to see that I was moving away from how things had been and was developing a new normal, a new approach to life.

I was beginning to function again. There were good days when I got everything done that needed to be done, and I had moments of clarity. There were still many days that I was depressed. I would slog through my duties and wonder when things would improve. And then there were setbacks like the trip to the burger shack.

One day about this same time, I was getting dressed for work. I grabbed my shirt and was surprised to find that something was on the shirt. It looked like a hardened purple booger. Just a fleck and then I noticed more flecks. All told I had fifteen flecks of purple booger on my shirt. I set the shirt aside and grabbed another shirt. Same story. I couldn't figure out what was on my clothes. I switched to a polo that I knew was clean and booger free. That evening I was working on getting my clothes in the wash to get the boogers cleaned and my son handed me a pair of jeans.

"Can you wash these? They're my favorite pair, and I want to wear them tomorrow."

"Sure," I said going through the pockets where I found a couple of crayons. Then it dawned on me. I asked my son why the crayons were in his pocket.

"I play a game with my friends at school to see if we can sneak crayons away from each other and put them in our pockets."

Apparently, a purple crayon had made it into the wash and, while in dryer mode, escaped from the pocket and landed all over my shirts. Now I had to buy more shirts so I had something to wear to work. I was going to need to buy a new wardrobe. Prior to this I would just ask my wife to go shopping with me and help me get something that would work. Let me be honest here. Like many guys, I'm most happy with an old, possibly stained grey T shirt with a couple of holes in it. That's what I wear when I'm relaxing. When I entered the program to get my master's degree, there was an evening when we went shopping. My wife selected some shirts that would look good with whatever pair of pants I chose to wear, and I always asked her if a tie worked with the shirt. I'm not a real fashion conscious person, but I know enough to know who to ask. She did a good job, too because many times I received comments from other teachers about how good my ties looked with my shirts. Now I had to choose for myself. I made my selections from an online store and waited for my clothes to arrive in the mail, all the while nervous about which ties I could get away with and which were too edgy. There were a couple ladies at work that I trusted to not laugh at me too long or loud, and I would show up in their classrooms first thing in the morning with ties in hand asking, "Which one is best?" Eventually I began making a list and checking it twice. Gonna remember which tie looks really nice.

It was one of these teacher ladies that helped me learn how to cook French toast. There's a reason she's a teacher because I can cook killer French toast. She texted me the instructions one wintry snow day morning during my first year without Sheryl. It was simple steps like this with direction from new friends that guided me as I began to rebuild my life.

The paradigm was still shifting. I was still struggling each day as I worked through my grief. I was still learning how to meet my needs. I was still not getting everything right, but I was also seeing some success. Some days it was only one little iddy biddy success, but it was an improvement. I'd take it.

I had been successful over spring break. We had a very enjoyable time and had spent our wet and rainy week in the camper, and I was beginning to think I could put together a longer trip. Maybe venture outside of Oregon and see some things. It also happened that my cousin had a daughter that was getting married in LA about the same time, so I invited my parents to accompany us on the first leg of our journey. I was also talking with an acquaintance who made a yearly migration to LA and a visit to Disneyland. He invited us to go with them. We were going to LA. Things were beginning to line up. I was beginning to form an itinerary, and plans were coming together. This trip would be the first of many trips, and we began keeping track of the many places we'd visited on a big map stuck on the wall of the camper with little stickers of each state we'd been to and the date. It was a highlight of each day to see where we'd been and to put that little sticker on the map. To the average person it might not seem important, but to me, making this journey was the first step in a new direction. The paradigm had been shifting and would continue to move, but now I was beginning to have some say over where it landed.

Putting the Pieces Together Again

Moving Past My Past

IT WAS SIX WEEKS THAT can't be replicated. We had a wonderful time every day. The first couple of weeks were spent in the greater LA basin. We explored many things. The second week was a trip to the Magic Kingdom, and then we were off to San Diego to spend a couple of days there catching up with an old Army buddy. Then we moved east towards the four corners area of the US. This included a trip to the Grand Canyon and stops along the way with yet another old friend that I hadn't seen in close to ten years and who had never met Tucker. Interspersed were many hours behind that wheel of my truck just working through my problems, sorting out life events and planning how I would deal with the next crisis. It wasn't formal, but I got my counseling just by logging miles, and the farther I drove, the farther my fears and struggles seemed to fall behind me. Our journey would eventually see us get all the way to Yellowstone Park before we headed for home.

Fresh Starts

At the end of the previous school year, I had run into trouble with my supervisor at work. He didn't like how I did things and was determined to run me out of education. While I was on my summer trip, he moved to a different school, and I was left to make corrections. My new supervisor told me on day one he didn't understand why I was in trouble. He didn't see the need for the corrective actions. A part of the plan was to write out in specific detail exactly what I would be doing each day and the theory behind each activity. It's very much like what I had to do when I earned my master's degree, and here I was, going through the motions all over again. I took the additional daily work as a means to improve my professional practice, and I think I made improvements. In my personal life, I went through the same steps.

I was beginning to adjust to a new reality. At work I had to justify my activities in class using the theory behind education. I began to apply the same mentality to rebuilding my life. The previous spring, my boss called me to his office to inform me that it would take a couple years, but that he would go through the steps needed to see me lose my license to teach. I was upset because I was trying my very best each day to improve my teaching and life skills and felt like I wasn't being supported in any way. Regardless, I took a philosophical approach in my response. Occasionally major league baseball players get sent back to the minor leagues. I might spend some time in the minors, but I would return to the majors, and he wouldn't be successful in his quest. I applied myself to improving me and was beginning to function and see small victories each day. I began to make edible meals consistently. At a basic level, I was beginning to understand how certain ingredients helped or hurt what I was doing. I was beginning to codify in my mind why I was doing what I was doing each day.

Why did I get up and enjoy some coffee before I started the process of getting ready for school? I did it because I liked the peacefulness of the new morning as dawn began to brighten the eastern horizon. Keep in mind, if I'm given a choice, I'll sleep in till noon, but if I have to get up for work, I might as well make it worth my time. Behind that was the idea of a fresh start. My life was full of fresh starts. So why not begin the new day with a fresh cup of coffee, too?

The Fog Lifts

In keeping with my newfound practice, I marked the passing of Sheryl's death. She died on her birthday, so I made sure I visited her grave on this first birthday since she passed. I was visiting Sheryl's grave because I wanted to, not because of a sense of duty, and not because I was guilted into the visit by someone else. Because of veteran privilege, I have a grave reserved for me at a national cemetery, and she is allowed to use the same grave that I do. The only real issue is that the cemetery isn't in my hometown; it's an hour away.

So, I took the day off and made the journey. I wanted to make this a day that would mark a new beginning. After getting my son to school I had a good breakfast at a favorite restaurant before heading out of town. Along the way I bought some flowers to place on her grave. I drove by a park that Sheryl enjoyed visiting and took steps to make the day special. Once I arrived at the cemetery, it took some searching to find where she was buried. One, it's a large cemetery, and two, I hadn't actually visited the grave site yet. This day would be the first of many trips. It was late September and unusually cold and rainy. The wind cut through my coat, quickly chilling me where I stood in front of the marker. As I remembered the events from previous years and reflected on how different my life had become, something unexpected happened. The clouds began to part and the rain stopped. As the sun began to shine brightly, I began to see colors once again. I hadn't even realized my view on life had been limited to various shades of grey. Looking back, I remember the day my vision changed. It was the day before Sheryl's brain surgery took place. We were exiting the hospital, and I sensed a dark tunnel consuming and overwhelming me, but now as the sun warmed me and filled the little valley where the grave lay, I began to see colors: bright blue sky that framed some brilliant white clouds, lush evergreen trees with other trees in full color as their leaves changed from green to yellow and red. I began to see my green car again. Just a few minutes earlier, it had been a dull grey. The marble of the gravestones seemed to glow and became whiter in the light. I didn't realize how much stress and grief had affected me. I didn't realize I had been so limited. Nature took on a newfound beauty that day.

I also began to think more clearly. Work began to fall into place. During the first year after Sheryl died, I couldn't think clearly enough to correctly form a good question. This is a necessary skill for teaching, but my fog had been complete. My practice had been to visit with a trusted co-worker and ask for his assistance. He was gracious and helped me without complaint, but now when I entered his classroom, I was coming with a completely formed question, and I asked for verification, not creation of a question. It was a start. I was making progress and mentally returning to the workforce.

Let me take a moment here and explain something. If you are in a supervisory role in your duties at work, give those under your supervision a measure of grace. When asked how I was doing that first year, I would respond with "I'm fine." I wasn't fine, but people don't want to hear the truth. They don't want to know what you're really going through. If you doubt my observation, the next time someone asks you how you are, respond with something like, "Oh you know, milk and a loaf of bread." I'm willing to bet the response will be something akin to "Oh good. That's good." As a society we don't really listen to what people say as a part of our greeting. My supervisor really didn't care how I was doing. If he had cared, he would have sat down and asked probing questions about how I was getting through each day. He didn't. Instead, I got glad-handed, and the topic moved on. There was no care and concern. If you have an employee or someone you supervise, and that person has a death in the family, give them all the space they need to recover from the loss. This will take months, not weeks or a few days. I was told to not make any major lifestyle decisions for at least a year. I would not be thinking clearly enough to process the decisions correctly, but my boss expected me to be one hundred percent on my game three weeks after the passing of my wife. I understand that some people can do that. I would also question the validity of a healthy marriage and wonder how long they had actually been together. Anyone I know who's had a healthy marriage isn't going to recover quickly. Healing takes time. So, give your employee the time to heal. And if you're in a position of making policy, then make the changes to benefit your employees. As a boss, you will reap the rewards by having fewer errors, and employees will return the favor and extend grace to you as a boss, making work life that much easier.

Planning Ahead

I was beginning to make strides in my personal life, too. Mornings became easier because I was doing a better job of planning. I was more aware of upcoming events with my son's school activities, and I began to make it a personal policy that lunches would be packed from home, and we wouldn't use the hot lunch program. There were two reasons for my change. One, it's cheaper to fix a peanut butter and jelly sandwich than buy a hot lunch. Two, if sack lunches were packed daily, then field trip days wouldn't be unusual, just another day to pack a sack. This helped avoid confusion and eliminated the need for someone to buy Tucker a lunch along the way. This was part of the changes I'd made on our trip from the summer. How would I approach each day? My goal was to be completely prepared every evening before I went to bed: sack lunches made, clothes set out so no decisions had to be made in the morning regarding what would be worn to school. It helped me as a parent be more successful in getting my son ready for each day. Because I was prepared the night before, I also had time to adjust to sudden changes, that curve that life tries to throw seemingly when we are unprepared. I didn't need another trip to the photo studio, so I avoided that kind of problem by planning.

Soccer Dad

I still had hurdles to overcome. Sports has always been a big part of my life, so when my son informed me that he wanted to participate in Pee Wee soccer, I fully supported him, but I wasn't prepared for the harsh reality that met me at the soccer pitch. I was a single dad, and Tucker didn't have a mom to cheer him on. Practice wasn't a problem, but game days were. I would set up my chair at the edge of the field, and it would be undisturbed if I didn't have to leave the immediate area, but on the first game day, Tucker had left his water bottle with me, and I needed to cross the field to get it to him. This left my chair unattended. By the time I returned to the parent side of the field, my belongings had been relocated to the back row. Yeah, that pushy soccer mom that haunts suburbia was planted firmly where my chair had been, and then she put up her beach umbrella blocking my view from the back row. I moved down the sideline, and I had a good view of the match, but soccer mom's little angel had no athleticism and kept kicking the ball to my son who would move it down field and score. Mom would then loudly announce to her kid that it wasn't their fault the other kid (my son) took the ball away from her angel. At one point, she even told the official that the goal should not be awarded (we weren't keeping score; it's a Pee Wee league) and the ball should be given back to her kid to kick. The ref shook his head in disbelief. A nearby mother whose son was a teammate to my son told this mother to shut up. I expected at this point that a fight would break out. The statement drifted across my mind, "I went to a Pee Wee soccer game and an MMA fight broke out." This could be cool. Soccer mom shut up, and we got to the end of the game. After the contest, my son headed my way, and the obnoxious mom loudly started her banter again telling her angel how terrible the player on the other team had been. "Good job son! You had a great game," I loudly proclaimed. Looking up from my son towards a glaring soccer mom, I broadly smiled fully expecting her to start in on me. This was unknown territory and being the only dad without an estrogen unit could be dangerous. I had watched parental pairings. Dad usually let mom handle any major disagreements. I figured that out in the first thirty seconds. Mom was in charge, and if mom wasn't happy, ain't nobody gonna be happy. I had a chat with my son on the way home from the game that day. I told him to not listen to anyone but his coach and me. Other moms didn't know what they were talking about, so he should ignore them while he was playing. He understood my point and let me know it. As I complain about others, I want to give credit where it is due. Regardless of the sport my son played, and regardless of the league, other moms always stepped up their support of my son. Sometimes it was in the form of a question, "Is Tucker's Mom gonna be at the game?" Other times they just seemed to figure it out, but it never took very long for the team moms to understand the situation, and they cheered him on just like they did their own. Regardless, I made it a policy to keep it cool and set up near one end of the playing field. We also set in place a policy that after a goal or a touchdown or any other excellent play, Tucker would look in my direction for a thumbs up! That meant YEAH!!! Awesome job!!! It was just a quiet dad and son thing. Since that first year, we have made friends, and Tucker signs up for sports he can play with his cousins. Unlike that first year, he now has many people cheering him on.

Life Happens Anyway

I had used my time that previous summer to set my priorities. During the previous years I had been letting life dictate to me the activities of the day. Life was setting the schedule, and I found myself waiting in fear for the next big catastrophe. I wasn't going to keep living that type of life. I was determined to dictate to life what would happen each day. This didn't always happen.

It was between classes, and I was outside my classroom door greeting students as they entered my class. I was bantering with another teacher and trying to keep things lighthearted before we got to the seriousness of the lesson. I didn't hear the phone ring, but I did hear the bell ring, and I entered my class.

"Hey folks, how ya doin'?"

Before a student could answer, the faceless voice from the intercom announced, "Mr. Strunk, your son's school called. I am sending a sub to your room. You need to go and get your son. He got hurt during recess."

"Oh crap! Okay, I'll get out of here and get him, thank you."

I turned to my class and informed them that the plans had changed for the day. I then directed them to the secondary assignment I had prepared. Remember, I had been in trouble with my supervisor. He seemed to think I wasn't doing a good job as a teacher, so I was forced to rethink how I would plan for each lesson. One of the adjustments I'd made was to have a backup plan. This is usually in the form of a larger project or an extended list of vocabulary terms that can be kept on a back burner and pulled out at a moment's notice, and that's what I did. It took thirty seconds to redirect my class to the alternate assignment, and as I finished my instructions, the sub walked through the door.

Tucker had been playing tag on the playground and, while at full gallop, was redirected into a metal tetherball pole. The way it was related to me was that his head was the first part of his body to make contact and then his arms and legs flew forward past the pole like a cartoon, and then he slid to the ground. What worried the school was that, as he slid to the ground, he slumped over and didn't move. The teacher on playground duty hurried over to check on him, and when she got to him, he began to stir. In other words, as he was running past a pole, another child gently pushed him sideways towards the pole. Because his leg was in motion, he couldn't stop the momentum and plowed into a metal pole, head first, knocking himself out. I've been around enough head injuries to know what the far-away look and slurred speech meant. When I arrived at his school, Tucker was in the main office, and he had the look. He was trying to focus on something far away.

"Hey Dauwd? Why... why...um...," he looked past me by about a thousand yards, "Why are you...um heresh?" I signed him out of school. As I was checking us into the urgent care clinic, he suddenly had a moment of cognition.

"Hey Dad, you know how I hurt my head?" His voice rang crystal clear.

"Yes, son, I do."

"I don't think I hurt the pole," he said in all seriousness that can be summoned only by a six-year-old with a concussion. The icy stare from the nurse could have reversed global warming.

"Well, that's good, son. I'm sure the pole appreciates your concern." I swallowed my smile and tried not to laugh out loud.

At home after the doctor's visit to confirm my suspicions, we were sitting on the couch watching a children's movie. It was a quiet afternoon. I reflected on the events of the day. Life had tried to overcome my plans, and to a certain degree, it succeeded. Any time a child gets a concussion is a bad day. I wasn't at school teaching. I was at home nursing a concussion, but the system of planning I had established over the course of the previous summer was in full operation. I took pride in the fact that my system had worked. Dinner was simple and only took a few minutes to prepare because I was planning ahead for just such an event.

Only a few short weeks later, life came at me hard yet again. It was almost our Christmas break and was cold out. Snow was a possibility if the warm, moist storm approaching our region couldn't dislodge the cold front that had us shivering in our boots. As it turned out, the warm moist air went up and over the cold locking our state in a deep freeze with moisture falling through the cold air. We were in the process of getting hit with a major winter blast. Because of transportation issues, the high schools for our district were some of the last schools to let out. My son had been dismissed from his school and was waiting for me to come and get him. A quick call from his school office to my school office got me out of work. As we headed home I made sure we got in a few cookies (sliding the car around an empty parking lot). We made a quick stop by the grocery store to get a few perishable things: milk, eggs, bread. It had already been snowing for a couple of hours when we climbed out of the car in our driveway. A short snowball fight later and groceries put away, we began to watch the news.

I should include here that we only get snow in our part of the world maybe every three or four years, and it's usually just a couple of inches. By the next day it's melted, and we don't see snow again for another three or four years, except for the rare storm where freezing weather gets trapped in our valley, warm moist air goes over the top and we get dumped on. Well–okay, getting dumped on means maybe six inches or so. We don't have any snow removal equipment because it would never get used, so when we actually get some build up, it's a big deal. We spent some time watching society struggle with the storm. Traffic was at a stand-still, and nobody was going anywhere. News reporters were frustrated because they had been trying to get to a predetermined location to report on the storm and had spent hours trying to get out of the parking lot. News organizations were announcing, "If you have a student that attends the following school districts, you need to leave work and go and get your child." Not that it would matter because the roads were jammed with people trying to get their kid and get home.

We got bored so we headed outside. We couldn't let a chance at a good snowball fight pass us by. We were having a lot of fun. While we were engaged in our battle, it had grown dark. Steam was boiling off of us and, in spite of the exertion, we grew cold. It was a great way to spend the afternoon and early evening. Once we got our wet clothes off, it was time for quick showers. This was also a part of the new plan. Get a shower when it works best. It doesn't have to wait until morning but could be taken in the evening like after a snowball fight. Warmed but hungry, I started dinner and turned on the TV. The situation across our region had only grown worse. It would be days before cars were removed from streets and society would begin to function again. Some people were struggling to get food or fuel for their cars. We were set. Because I had planned ahead and had food in storage, we only needed a few perishables to get us by. We spent the next few days enjoying the freedom of not having to go to school.

Twice in just a few short weeks, events outside of my control, what I call "life," could have completely derailed not just an afternoon or a day but days on end. I was seeing my pre-planning beginning to work. The average person reading this would probably think this is stupid, and before my wife got sick, before that afternoon trip to the photo studio, I would have agreed, but my life had gone through some major changes. I was now the only person to care for my son. If we needed groceries or if we didn't have something in the house, it was because I'd failed in my responsibilities as a parent. If I failed at my responsibilities, my son would suffer the consequences. I wanted the best for my son, so I had to step up and provide the best, and I did. I had moved past my past and was making a better future for my son.

The New Normal

We finished up the school year without any other major incidents. It was a good year, all things considered, but what would we do with our summer? I wanted to get away from my house. I wanted to hit the open road, get away and leave my troubles behind me. Circumstances kept me in town for the majority of the summer. The only travel I was able to squeeze in was a weekend trip to Idaho. Not really a major trip, but I did spend many hours that summer organizing my house and getting things cleaned up. Life as I had known it has never returned to "normal." A new normal has replaced the old.

While I was married, I always had a spouse I could rely on to cover the parts of life I couldn't get to, and I could cover parts of life that she couldn't get to. When we got home from work, we would have many things to do and a little time to get them all accomplished, but I could be working on one task while my wife worked on a different task. After dinner, Sheryl could get our son a bath while I did the dinner dishes. That way after Tucker got to bed, we could sit and relax and not have any chores still needing to be performed, but with Sheryl's passing, I didn't have anyone to tag team with. At the end of the day when we arrived home, dinner still needed to be made.

The house needed to be cleaned. Laundry needed to be put in the washer/dryer/folded. Tucker needed a shower. Lunches needed to be made for the next day. Homework, if assigned, needed to be completed, and while doing all of those things, I needed to keep track of a small child. Time was my enemy, and managing time became my number one priority for getting through each day. I have exactly the same amount of time in any day that Henry Ford or Louis Pasteur had: 24 hours, but I found that I couldn't get everything done. If I had to work in the yard, I couldn't be working on dinner prep. If I had to fold laundry, I couldn't be getting my bills paid. I learned or created shortcuts to shave time off my required chores. I did things like mix the entire jar of jelly with peanut butter so that when it came time to make lunches all I had to do was spread this emulsion instead of many different parts. It may sound ridiculous, but those few minutes saved meant I had more time to complete other things. Another adjustment I made was to wear colored denim jeans to work. Yes, I would still wear some blue jeans, but I also included black and tan and grey into the mix. I would pair these with polo shirts made from a performance fabric instead of cotton which might need an iron. I watched closely which casual shirts wrinkled quickly and which resisted wrinkles. I quit buying shirts from manufactures that didn't make wrinkle resistant fabric. I no longer needed to iron my clothes unless I was going to wear slacks and a dress shirt. I also reverted to a trick I'd picked up in the military. Once a month I'd add starch to the creases of the sleeves on my dress shirts. This made the crease semi-permanent. After a few applications I didn't need to iron the sleeves as long as I hung up the garment while it was still warm. The semi-permanent crease would look like I'd ironed a crease into the sleeve. I switched from buying blocks of cheese to pre-shredded cheese. It might carry a higher price tag, but it saved me time. In spite of all these changes, I still failed to get everything done like I wanted to. There were always things to remind me of how much my life had changed.

The Garden

The year I put in an RV pad next to my driveway was the year I put in raised garden beds in the backyard. I was excavating many wheelbarrows full of dirt and that dirt became my garden. Vegetables always taste better when they've just been picked from the garden, and we enjoyed many meals from our garden. When Sheryl got sick, the original plan was that she would defeat cancer and normalcy would ensue. What better way to move us towards a long life than by planting vegetables in the garden. New life equals a new lease on life. We had endured the Saturday that took us to the photo studio, but there were still two days left in the holiday weekend. It was planting time, and I made sure that my seeds found soil. I made a place for Sheryl to sit peacefully amongst the tools and packets of seed and made sure she got just a brief misting from the hose as we watered in the seeds. It was a late spring day and the warmth brought out the full scent of blooming trees. Planting the garden would be the last activity that we would do together as just the three of us: Mom, Dad, Son. That evening as I helped Sheryl prepare for her battle against cancer, the yard was mowed and weeded and a new garden was planted. We were starting fresh. I had hope that the yard work would signal a new beginning for us, and that Sheryl would be delivered yet again from cancer.

Two days later, we arrived at the hospital early. Sheryl was on the schedule as the first patient for the day. Twelve hours later she would be wheeled into recovery and would begin the week-long stay in the hospital to get her back on her feet. My days were filled with making sure she was comfortable and cared for by the nurses and doctors. I would arrive early in the morning, usually before 7AM and most nights would still be by her side when visiting hours ended at 9PM. My son was spending the week with his grandparents, so all I had to do was let the cat in at night and get him fed. All my energies that week were spent at the hospital. I totally forgot about the garden. Because of a light rain a couple of nights that week the plants got a little water. And I remembered the following weekend to get them a drink, but the garden took a back seat to everything else going on in our lives. It was only a matter of a couple of weeks before the effects of chemo and radiation took their toll on Sheryl and she wound up in the hospital too weak to lift her head off the pillow. At the same time my garden suffered. I didn't water it. I didn't weed it. I didn't trim off some of the blooms. It was left to grow wild. As we lived through the events of that summer my garden didn't fare well. By the time Sheryl passed away, the garden had been completely overgrown and scorched brown. At some point, it had failed to exist due to neglect. I can justify all day long about how that garden wasn't important and was the least of my concerns and in the long run really didn't matter a whole bunch, but that garden also represented the death of what my life had been.

As fall set in that first year after Sheryl's death I didn't remove the dead plants. I didn't care for the soil. I did nothing to care for the garden. Sometime mid-winter after a strong wind storm blew through the region, I realized that there wasn't a single plant left in the garden. The wind had carried them all away, which meant that someone somewhere wound up with a bunch of dead pea plants on their front porch. The garden area was barren soil and soon weeds would begin to grow. The neighborhood cats also loved the garden because it was soft soil and perfect for digging in to use as a litter box.

That garden also represented the changes that happened to me emotionally. Life before Sheryl's passing was full. It was vibrant and like the scripture in Psalm 23, a green pasture. I would get out into the garden and weed and trim away blossoms to encourage growth and water morning and night. When the plants brought forth their yield, I would listen to the joy of finding new growth as my wife and son explored. I would enjoy a meal that included a green salad full of fresh vegetables that were less than an hour from being on the vine. I would enjoy family time.

But now that garden had died and been replaced with a litter box. I saw my life the same way. I no longer had the resource of time to plant or care for a garden. My meals would consist of frozen vegetables from a bag.

There was no more joy, no more refreshment, no more vibrancy. I had been living a Psalm 23 green pasture life. Instead of being led to a celebratory table, I felt like I had been led into a barren desert. Every time I looked at the raised garden beds, I saw the reality of how barren life had become. When we arrived home at the end of the day, it was a race to get dinner on the table and get a shower in and get to bed before it got too late. We no longer had time to play a game or watch a cartoon together. If we watched any TV together it was during our dinner. The closet filled up with games we used to play but no longer had the time for. We had settled into a routine, but it lacked life.

It took me a few months to figure out what was happening, but I began to notice a pattern. I would get my son after school and he would be happy and talkative and excited about life. As soon as we started down our street, he would become quiet and grumpy, and by the time we made it to the front door, he was angry. About what, he didn't know. To his young mind it was beyond explanation. He was just angry. I was usually trying to figure out how I wasn't going to spoil dinner, so I was distracted and not really paying attention to what was going on. Eventually, as the evening wore on, his attitude would improve and we would have peace. I was also struggling with lighting my house. Maybe it's just an emotional thing, but once Sheryl entered the hospital for brain surgery I could never get enough light in my house. I could open every blind and curtain and turn on every light and it was still dark in my house. I replaced every light bulb with the strongest bulb I could find, and still I felt like I was stumbling around in the dark. Even though life had achieved a sense of normalcy, and a routine had developed, it wasn't a fulfilled life. It was barren and lifeless just like the litter box in my backyard that had once been a lush garden.

Reminders

We lived for summer and other breaks from school. We couldn't always have a six or eight week vacation, some summers we needed to stay local and save our money, but the following summer we would be gone for many weeks. As a result of our long vacations, we explored the western part of the US. One summer vacation we visited eight national parks or monuments, each one in a different state, in six weeks. Summer trips were the best part of our year. On the road to our next vacation spot, we were free from all the reminders that haunted us as we lived our daily lives back home. If we lacked the funding for a long trip we made numerous three and four day trips to the nearby coast or mountains. Eventually, summer would end, and we would need to return to school. I would try my best to get Tucker all excited about the new things he would learn that year in school, and that excitement lasted about three days before we would settle back into the same routine.

It took years for me to realize that I was avoiding certain areas of my home and yard. I had reworked the bedroom that had served as Sheryl's hospice room. That room had become a storage room. If we had junk or old furniture or anything we didn't know what to do with, it was stuffed into that room. I cleaned out that room and changed the color from pink to blue. Once the covid lockdowns started, I was relegated to that bedroom for zoom meetings and classes, but I hated being in that room. I also never went into my backyard. That was where the garden was located. I would cook from a BBQ grill on my patio, but I stayed away from one end of the patio because you could see the garden area. I tore down the boxes that made up the garden area and paid someone to level the soil. I could never bring myself to plant a garden again. Too many memories surrounded the activity. I needed to move away from my house. I felt that when my wife had passed, it was best for us to stay in the same house for a sense of continuity. I felt it was best to help us move on. Those who counseled me told me to not make any fast decisions, wait at least a year. It had been four or almost five years at this point, and I realized it was time to get us moved. Memories were encroaching on life. Memories had been weighing us down and causing us to dwell in the past and not look to the future. It would take another three years before we could get moved. The many things that needed to be completed also competed for my time and energy.

Old Friends

About this same time, I reconnected with a couple of old Army buddies. When I was prowling around Germany, we connected. These people think like I do, act like I do and laugh at exactly the same things I do. In a phrase, we were made for each other. We hadn't been in contact for decades, but we reconnected. Using modern technology, we stay in contact by texting each other every day. If I haven't heard my phone chirp in a few hours I'll get on it and see what's going on in their lives, and they do the same with me. We have a conversation thread that is years old. We live thousands of miles apart, but I am closer to these old friends than I am to anyone else. Life has been hard for each of us, so we understand the struggles with each day. We encourage each other daily. It isn't a stretch to know that everyone needs a friend. I've had friends or people that I thought cared about me, but in the end I wound up with no one in my corner. No one to talk to. No one to get a cup of coffee with. Now I have people that truly care about me. They will confront me if they think I'm not living up to my potential. They will challenge me to do better. Many times, they have received a text from me as I vent my frustrations. They are an answer to prayer. In the book of Ecclesiastes, scripture talks about needing friends. "Two are better than one, because they have a good return for their labor: If either of them falls down, one can help the other up, but pity anyone who falls and has no one to help them up."1 Friends carry one another's burden. If you stumble, a friend helps you get up. Simply by being a friend we help each other overcome the challenges in life. Crying with you or laughing with you. If you have a concern about life, they are there to listen to your fears, concerns, burdens. I have seen where married people are closer to their friends than their own spouse. Who do they spend their free time with? The friend. The spouse gets the leftover spare time. It works for some couples anyway. I always wanted my wife to be my closest friend, but now that I don't have a spouse, I really needed these friends. I'd been living a life void of friends. If I got down or lonely, I had no one to help me get up. My guitar, and music, provided my solace. By reconnecting with old friends,

I had others who even though they didn't live near, were always available to help keep me on an even plane emotionally. I still faced challenges every day. Life didn't suddenly get any easier. I still have to show up for life, but now I had others to help me face those challenges.

I shouldn't have been surprised. If encouragement came from anyone, it would be these friends. One day my phone chirped and I read the text.

"I needed to share this with you. Your life's gonna get better. 'See, I am doing a new thing! Now it springs up; do you not perceive it? I am making a way in the wilderness and streams in the wasteland.' Isaiah 43:19" [1]

My friends knew my struggles. They understood where I was emotionally and how I struggled with daily reminders of my past life. They also knew that my life was going to undergo some changes.

And Another Thing

Let's recap what's happened so far. I was happily married with a good career, pretty wife, a young child, and we were trying for a second. My wife loses a three-year battle with cancer, and I get to pick up the pieces of a shattered life while raising my son. My friends who did an amazing job of carrying me during my time of crisis have drifted away, and I spent months without anyone to share my fears, concerns, joys, triumphs, and dreams. I have read scripture that says I've been through rich times in my life and a dark valley. That scripture says I should be seated at a celebration table. Instead I felt like God in all His might and wisdom has led me into the wilderness and left me in the dust. I have old friends that I've reconnected with who encourage me and have told me they think great changes are coming my way. Have I missed anything?

Yes. The anger. I was disappointed about where life had left me, and I was angry. Not in a violent, I'm gonna shoot up society type of way, but a deep resentment that left a sharp edge on my view of reality. The idea that if something bad was gonna happen, something irritating, it would happen to me.

Saturday is my day to run errands, and this particular week my Saturday was extremely full. We finally made it to the grocery store in the late evening. Sunday passed without any problems until after Tucker went to bed, and I began to prepare for Monday. As a part of our bedtime preparations, I asked my son to lay out his clothes for the next morning.

"Dad I don't have any shorts for school. I need clothes washed." I had been so busy I forgot to get laundry in the wash. Not a problem. I could do a combined load and get enough things washed that we could get through one day, and I'd get laundry caught up on Monday evening. Okay, crisis averted. Lunches were prepared except for the sandwiches. I'd get those done later after Tucker went to bed. An hour later, I grabbed the necessary ingredients to make sandwiches, but when I put the bread on the cutting board it was green. It was a brand new loaf I purchased the day before. I was vexed. Now to the average married person, this isn't a game changer. It just means that someone needs to make a grocery run, but I had a six year old who'd just fallen asleep. I wasn't going to wake him up to go to the store. I also wasn't going to leave him all by himself. I had to go with plan B. Only plan B meant making Mac 'n Cheese. Have I said how much I loathe Mac 'n Cheese? Vexed was left in the past. I'm moving past irked. When I got out the makings for Mac 'n Cheese, I didn't have any milk. It was still on my list. I had failed to get any at the store. Did I say I was irked? No, I've become highly agitated! The thought crossed my mind, Why Me? What did I do to deserve this?

In my calm state, I can recognize my thinking errors here. This sort of thing happens to everyone. As a married person without a kid, there were times I went to the store late in the evening because we needed a grocery item so lunches could be made. This current situation was no different in any way. I simply had failed to plan out and set in place everything I needed for this particular evening. It shouldn't have been a big deal, but I had held onto this deep resentment. It was me against the world. Eventually, I was able to think clearly and make some choices and we had spaghetti for lunch. My son thanked me for the special treat. If only he had known it wasn't plan A.

Drive Therapy

The school year was ending, and I was in for more steering wheel counseling on yet another summer vacation. This vacation was special in many ways. At the time we wouldn't know it, but it would be our last camping adventure across the vastness of the Western US. We visited Dodge City in Kansas, home to many tales from western folklore. Being a history teacher, I truly loved to visit this place. We would get to visit Texas and the gulf coast. Something I'd always wanted to do but had never been able to find the time to accomplish. Now I would get to, and I would get to spend an amazingly awesome week with my Army Buddies! I also realized I needed to let go of things that were bothering me.

In her last few months of life, Sheryl would make hurtful statements. I don't know of anyone else who received this treatment from her, but I got to experience it on a regular basis. Sheryl was deeply affected by cancer. Her biggest complaint was that because of the side effects of chemo, we couldn't have any more children. She was bitter about this to her dying day. I have reflected on some of the statements that she made, and I think she was mad at me over the misinterpretation of my actions. When she was sick, I tried to make her life as comfortable as possible, but we didn't get any alone time. We didn't sit and talk through things or what might be possible outcomes. Later as she was dying, I tried to meet her needs and keep everything functioning like it had. One day in particular stands out because I had to pick up the toys not once or twice, but three times, because visitors had let their kids drag out Tucker's toys, and when they left my house, they didn't pick up after themselves.

I hadn't yet adjusted to changes in my mind. The last time I was able to sit and have a conversation with my wife was the morning of the trip to the photo studio, and that was interrupted. If we'd taken more opportunities to talk, I think much of the person-to-person hurt wouldn't have happened. I think those hurtful statements would have been identified as lashing out from a sense of helplessness. Too many times I've had people ask me for advice on what should be done because they have a spouse who's dying from cancer. I tell them to spend time talking with their spouse. Don't just function and get things done. Talk through the hurt and helplessness.

It's easy to say just talk through the problems, but harder to do when put into practice. Many evenings while Sheryl was undergoing chemo, I would get home from work, and she would be asleep on the couch. I would coordinate meal delivery and clean the house. I would try to keep my son quiet and in another room so we wouldn't disturb Sheryl while she was sleeping. I kept myself very busy just keeping up with the status quo. Only later, after nearly killing myself with the work, did I understand that as life had shifted, so had the status quo. My expectations should also have shifted. No one sat me down and said, "It's okay to let things go." I did not allow myself this grace until months later when I wound up in the hospital needing emergency surgery. If I had given myself that measure of grace before Sheryl passed, I would have sat with her, just to be a comfort, while she was asleep. I would have had those needed conversations that would have brought her peace about our survival after her passing. I was too busy keeping the house clean and doing laundry and other chores to spend time with my wife. When she needed reassuring I was in the other room completing a task. I prided myself on the fact that her physical needs were met, but I wasn't meeting her emotional needs.

The result was that we didn't talk, and Sheryl responded with anger and bitterness. That bitterness spilled over into her attitude towards me, and there were many evenings I could do nothing right. Some of this may have been the result of the cancer growing deep within her brain and changing her personality and feelings. I don't have an expert opinion, but whatever the source of it, she took it all out on me, and I never had the chance to say my goodbyes. I hosted many people in my house during her last days—an amazing experience—but I got left out. Some say this is very common.

As I began our trip that summer I was still nursing the emotional scars from this time. Somewhere between Abilene and the Texas Gulf Coast, a voice inside my head asked me why it all mattered. Will any of it make a difference in the end? How was I going to change anything if I continued to harbor and in some cases, nurse that hurt back to life. I needed to let it go, and along the way, let the anger go, too. I could no longer allow it to be a controlling force in my life.

I was holding onto hurt directed at me possibly because I was the closest and most trusted. We didn't get time together, so I didn't know why I was on the receiving end of all the anger, and even though I was, what did it matter now anyway? Sheryl was gone. I had moved past my past and built a new normal. I was surging forward making a new life on my own. As I drove past mile after mile, I unpacked this emotional baggage and mentally left it alongside the road. I was free of the hurt and pain, and because I don't know exactly where I left it, and I can't go back and get it. Every self-help book I've read, and yes, I was given many, want to wrap up grief counseling as easy to package. It's so simple: just pack up these feelings and move on. Now don't you feel better? I disagree with most of those books. This isn't an easy adjustment. This isn't a one-stop solution to all my problems.

Comfort for the Survivor

Do Words Matter?

IT WAS THE FIRST FRIDAY night after I'd returned to work. It was late in the football season, and we were playing a team that was a cross-town rival. I arranged for someone to spend the evening with my son, and I ventured out socially for the first time in nine months. Many of my co-workers greeted me warmly as I made my way to the football stadium. It had been a long time since I had been in contact with most of them, and they wanted to catch up and see how I was doing, pass along their condolences, offer any help they could. One conversation led to another, and it was half time before I could get more than fifteen feet past the gate and into the stadium. In fact, that night I never did make it into the seats. Instead, I spent the time reconnecting. One conversation stands out from that evening.

A former student and football player that I'd coached had undergone a major change in his life as he stepped forward in his faith. He was in college and would be going to seminary to be an evangelist. He seemed troubled when he greeted me near the concession stand.

"I spent many hours praying for your wife's healing, and I don't understand why she died. I'm so sorry. I really prayed hard and expected that she would be delivered. I prayed really hard for her healing. I just don't understand."

His statement caught me off guard. For the first time in that conversation, I really looked at him and fully took in his countenance. He was troubled. Tears filled his eyes and began to spill down his cheeks. I began to tear up just from his intensity. I thanked him for his concern and passion. We talked about healing and how, when someone goes to heaven, they really get fully healed. I told him that God had answered his prayers, and he took comfort in my words, but at the same time, I examined my own words. How many times had I prayed that same prayer? "Lord please heal this person." How many times had I been disappointed when they died?

Our words matter. How we say things matters. I have found that people who haven't yet experienced life-disrupting trials don't know the words to say, but at the same time, they want to reassure me and make me feel better. Often they've not taken the time to invest in the situation. They want to spew something that sounds spiritual and move on so they can feel good about themselves, that they lifted me up without getting into the messy emotional details. The earnestness with which my former football player spoke to me during that brief conversation demonstrated his faith walk and how much he cared. It wasn't empty platitudes but a deep hurt within his own soul for my wife's life and my well-being. His pain was palpable. His caring was real. I expect he will be a great leader within the church because he really cares for people.

Miserable Comforters

During this transformative journey in my life, I have received troubling advice. That advice was that I was not living my life correctly or that Sheryl was guilty of a sin that she needed to confess, and then she would be delivered and live a long life. I've even had people quote James 1:2-4 to my face:

> "Consider it pure joy, my brothers and sisters, whenever you face trials of many kinds, because you know that the testing of your faith produces perseverance. Let perseverance finish its work so that you may be mature and complete, not lacking anything." 1

The Christian version of one-stop shopping for solutions. Let me be perfectly clear: Scripture is never wrong, but it can be applied incorrectly. These phrases don't bring comfort. They don't heal the hurt. They are empty words often spoken by someone who hasn't yet dealt with truly hard times. People will be sure to tell you how hard their lives are. They are the first to ask for deliverance because the car broke down or they didn't get the job they wanted, but when it comes to providing real comfort, their words fall short. Here's the point: It's not always going to be alright. Can God make all things all right? Yes, but we should remember that everything falls under His authority and His plans, not our plans. Isaiah 55:8-9 puts it this way:

> "For my thoughts are not your thoughts, neither are your ways my ways," declares the Lord. "As the heavens are higher than the earth, so are my ways higher than your ways and my thoughts than your thoughts." 1

Nowhere in this passage does it say anything about my plans super-seding God's plans or that everything is going to be okay. When Sheryl was diagnosed with cancer, I had been in a pretty happy frame of mind. It had taken me years to reach my goals. I was content. All was well in my world. I just needed to maintain the status quo, and all would continue to be well. Nowhere did it say God was going to change everything, but He didn't have to send me a note letting me know. He is God. Things play out on His timeline.

Name It and Claim It?

It was the first Sunday after we had been informed that the cancer had returned. We attended our Sunday school class at our church like we always did and told those present what was going on and what we knew. One dear saint immediately pops off with "Oh don't worry, everything is going to be alright." Seriously? What had this lady just heard? Didn't she hear me tell those present that the cancer had returned? Sheryl had six months to a year to live, and there was nothing that could be done about it. Yet here is this church lady telling us that we've got it all wrong. Had I missed something? Nope. This lady was a victim of modern day thinking in Christian circles: If I believe it, then God in all His mighty wisdom will see things my way and I, we, you will be delivered. I don't see this as being reality. God doesn't need us to make up His mind for Him. He's God, and He has a plan that is going to be so much better than what I could ever imagine. To think otherwise is to challenge God's sovereignty and is an attempt to replace His plans for our lives with our own.

I saw this played out in a similar situation. A young lady was dying from congenital heart disease. It was a condition she had lived with her entire life. It was expected that she would die young, but she lived her life as the disease would let her live. She outlived the expectations of the medical community. Because she was on the transplant list, everyone was excited when she got the call to immediately get to the hospital. Surgery was performed by the world's expert on heart transplants. Everything should have led to an exalted finish. Only the new heart wouldn't beat correctly. The term used was a *stone heart*. Because she was still technically in surgery she was still on the heart lung bypass but was needing massive blood transfusions. As hours turned into days, doctors couldn't get her heart to beat correctly. Plans were laid to pull the plug and let her die, but throughout the entire ordeal her parents claimed that God would deliver her. It was all a part of His plan. Let me be clear here, I believe that if God had willed it to happen, she could immediately have been healed and walked out of the hospital and run a full triathlon, but that didn't happen. God had other plans.

The same was true for Sheryl. Sheryl tried to live out her faith everyday as an example to others at her work. Her door was always open to anyone who needed to talk, and I've been told that she routinely shared her faith with others. Due to her work responsibilities, she had contact with every employee from every department. We held her memorial service on a Saturday so everyone could attend including many coworkers and their families. An estimated two hundred people from her work attended and filled about half of one section of the church. I made sure that her memorial service included her beliefs on faith. A few weeks later, I heard that all of the Bibles from the section where her coworkers sat were gone. One person estimated it was about eighty Bibles. I'm not saying this was the reason Sheryl had to die, but it was certainly a response to her passing.

I was questioning God during this time. What had I done to deserve my fate? Why was my son being punished by not having a mom? I was so deeply into the trial that I didn't even recognize it as a trial. This was just a difficult time. I didn't sit quietly at night saying to myself, "Well God, I can clearly see how your ways are higher than mine. Thank you so much for the trial. I know I'll be stronger because of it." There is a time and place for this kind of discussion, perhaps a Bible study or a Sunday school where the topic is clearly announced ahead of time so that people who are struggling with a similar situation can opt out of attending. You shouldn't have to sit through a lecture about how blessed your situation is while also dealing with the object of the lesson.

Wait for It

During the first four months of the entire cancer ordeal, one particular incident has stood out as a perfect example regarding words and how people use words to comfort others. We were walking out of the church service, and the usher who is an acquaintance of ours pulled me aside.

"Hey, I'm so sorry your wife has cancer and all that she's going through, but God has a blessing for you in all of this. I know cause I had cancer when I was young."

The surprise registered on my face.

"It's hard to see right now because of all you're dealing with, but God will give you a blessing as a result of what you're going through. Wait for it, and you'll see it."

I waited. And waited. And waited. Someone who was diagnosed with cancer sought me out and asked me questions about what was awaiting them in treatment. I waited some more. Time was passing. I didn't see any blessing. My wife got sick again, and this time she died. I still waited for the blessing. I didn't see it. A coworker asked me about breast cancer and what to expect if the test results came back positive. What were the possible outcomes? Then a few weeks later it was, "My grandma is dying of cancer. Can you talk with my family about your experiences?"

I soon started to see the blessing. It took a couple years before I began to see it. It wasn't anything I got other than the good feelings of being able to help others who were facing cancer. I wasn't a trained counselor who would charge them a fee for advice. I was just someone they could call up and yell at when needed. I was someone who understood their concerns and fears. I was someone who had wandered through the cancer battle with a loved one and was available to answer questions. I went to the hospital with a coworker whose cousin was dying of cancer at a young age. I sat quietly in the hallway while they said their goodbyes. Once the visit was over we made our way to a nearby coffee shop, and I listened as all the fears and bitterness and questions came out. I sat with my friend while they talked through the death of their loved one. A week or so later they visited my classroom during my prep period and thanked me for what I had done. As events would play out, the cousin had died a few hours after our visit. My coworker became the rock that the rest of the family had leaned on during the days leading up to the funeral service. I was given the credit for making it happen. I began to see a pattern and the blessing.

Looking back at that brief conversation held in the back of the church, I have just a couple of thoughts. First, I wasn't glad-handed and told that it would be alright. I was struggling with my wife's cancer just like she was, only my struggle was emotional, not physical. His comments were reassuring. He told me that he was a cancer survivor. That gave me hope. Not everyone dies from cancer. Second, it gave me a reason to look away from my circumstance. I began to watch for the blessing. This took my eyes off of my immediate struggle and away from the "woe is me" attitude that tried to take over. I don't think that was the intention of the conversation. I think the reason he said what he said was to provide comfort and to reassure me, and it did, but there were also additional positive results from that brief encounter.

It's part of our humanity that we want people to care for us, and we want to care for others. We want to connect with others and feel like we matter. One way we do that is to check in with them to see how they are doing. If I'm dealing with a most difficult issue like a spouse dying from cancer, I want my friends to ask me about my spouse and about me. What are the struggles of the day? Where are my emotions? What are my challenges?

In the weeks leading up to my wife's death, I spent many days visiting my favorite coffee joint. One day, the barista asked me about my wife, and as I explained her situation, he responded that in the same situation, he would be really angry at life. I explained to him just how angry I really was. He took the time to care. No one else ever asked me if I was angry. No one else asked about my emotions. Maybe they could tell I was really angry deep down inside, but this barista took the time to ask and to reassure. One person asked me to let them know if I was considering suicide, but I can't remember anyone else asking me anything similar. The focus was entirely on my wife and her struggles.

A Time for Everything

When Sheryl was sick I had a group text that was kept for months so that others who were most important to us were kept in the information loop, but when people stop checking in on us, then the pendulum swings the other way, and we feel like nobody cares. We feel lonely. So, as we come into contact with friends and coworkers and acquaintances throughout the day, it's normal for us to ask how others are doing. This is usually in the form of a greeting, a conversation starter. We want others to have positive feelings towards us. That's why we smile when we see someone we know. The same holds true for trying to encourage others. When they leave our presence, we want them to feel a need to visit again. We don't want them to avoid us because we make them feel bad, but it seems a lot of church people feel the need to have you leave their presence feeling totally upbeat and excited about life. Accordingly, if you are struggling in any way, you have a spiritual problem. You must leave their presence energized and happy, or they have failed, not just as a person, but spiritually, too. Many times, when I was tending to Sheryl as she lay dying in bed, I had church people stop on the way out of my house to pray with me that I would find joy in my trial. Joy in the death of my spouse? Really? Why can't I hurt? Why can't I be sad? How will I know what true joy is if I'm always joyful? If I'm allowed to be sad or grieve for a season, then when I do have joy, it will be real joy. Instead, we settle for a fake joy that in the end actually robs us of joy. We're so busy trying to fake it that we miss it completely.

Shouldn't the church embrace these differences, too? I often hear this name-it-and-claim-it philosophy. God wants me to be successful. Therefore, God has a big house and fancy car for me to drive. I've got to have the biggest and best of everything. I once heard a church person utter the phrase, "God has made us wealthy because He knows I love to shop." It was hard to hear. It seemed the person didn't even consider that maybe God had made them wealthy so they could bless others. This doesn't mean we have to live in a shack and be poor, but do we have to have a mansion when an average house will support our needs? Do we need a fancy car when an average car will do? Don't misunderstand the point. If you're well-to-do, I'm happy for you, but do we need big fancy things to be happy? Is my spiritual temperature determined by the square footage of my house? Base price of my car? The expensive suit I may or may not wear? Can I have a season where I'm sad, or do I always have to be happy? This matters. I know people who have walked away from their faith because of a perceived failure and judgement by church people. They quit church because they felt like they didn't measure up, but isn't that the point of church anyway? We don't measure up so we need God to forgive us. Why should there be a required joy component added to this?

When my wife was sick and in the months following her death, most of the encounters I had were with people trying to cheer me up. I didn't want to be cheered up. I wanted to grieve, but it seemed like their mission was simply to make me feel better and cheer me up. Many promises were made, but there was little follow up. A couple of notable encounters stand out.

I happened to run into a friend of mine who lived in a distant community while shopping at a large electronics store that was a considerable distance from my house. I asked about events in his life, and he asked me how I was doing. He was a distant person in my life but close because he was a pastor and had been giving me some casual counseling as I navigated my way through life. I knew he was concerned with my well-being, but also knew I could be sad in his presence. We talked for a couple of minutes, and then he told me, "It's okay to be sad and to grieve. It's okay. If we are still having this conversation in a few months or a couple of years, then maybe we need to talk more about being sad, but for now that should be expected. You're doing okay." A small burden lifted off my shoulders as I went about my shopping.

About this same time, I went to a meeting at work. There were supposed to be four of us at the meeting, and we were supposed to be planning the next unit quiz. Two of the four would be sick that day which was fine. I really didn't feel like doing the work that day anyway. Just in case our boss happened by, we remained "in the meeting" so he could see that we were hard at work. We solved many issues that morning, none of which had anything to do with a quiz. Eventually, the conversation came around to me and how was I adjusting to life. I explained that I was developing my skills as a cook and that Saturday mornings were filled with Pee Wee basketball. We each shared some funny stories related to little guy sports, and I felt like we made good use of our time just getting to know each other a little better. As the "meeting" ended, I made my way towards the classroom door, and my coworker and friend said something that I will never forget.

"I've never gone through what you're going through. And I'm sorry you have to deal with your spouse dying. I'm not gonna pretend that I know or understand what you're going through. And I'm glad I don't because I like my life the way it is. So, I won't ever pretend that I have an answer for you, but I do want you to know that I consider you my friend. And as your friend, I will help you in any way I can, and if you ever need help with anything, please ask. Cause as your friend, I want to help you.

Finally, someone who was being honest. I thanked him and reassured him that if there was ever anything I needed help with, I would be sure to ask. When I returned to my classroom, I sank into my desk chair, and the tears began to flow. It felt so good to have someone be honest with me. He wasn't trying to make me happy. I didn't have to leave the conversation joyful. I was given permission to have problems and hard days, but I knew that if I had a bad day, I could rely on my friend to help me through it. That was such a comfort especially in my time of deep need. Months later in a similar conversation, I told him how important that calm reassurance was to me. I told him how much of an impact it had on my life.

Assume Nothing

Do words matter? Does it matter how we say things? Absolutely! How I say things as a teacher can build up a student or hurt a student. An example is when I'm asking questions to check for understanding at the end of a lecture.

The eager student raises their hand, and they respond with an answer that is completely wrong, or maybe half right. I can say, "incorrect," or "not even close," or "were you listening to the lecture?" Or I can say, "not the answer I'm looking for." This very scenario wrongly played out in the classroom when I was getting my master's degree and license to teach, only I was the student.

On day two of our classes, the ultimatum was issued. We were to produce a detailed thesis regarding our philosophy on instruction in the classroom. I spent some hours thinking this question over. No one had ever asked me for my opinion of such matters. It was a Friday, and I had the weekend to work on my paper. I began to write. I started with my arguments and created what I thought to be a strong thesis. I gave examples for each argument and crafted what I thought was a tight paper. We were limited to six pages, and I filled each page with details of how my philosophy would play out in practice. Paper completed, I happily turned in my work on Monday morning. Tuesday came at me fast, and I settled into my seat eagerly working on my second cup of coffee. I expected class to begin with a lecture over the chapter that we had to read in our textbook. Instead, the professor launched into a tirade over the use of discipline in the classroom.

"We are not disciplinarians, we are teachers. And if we expected to maintain a career, we had better learn that disciplining a student was the responsibility of the parent." With that statement he pompously snatched my philosophy paper from his lectern and marched to my seat, slapped my work down on the desktop for the rest of the class to see. The giant, eight inch, red felt-tip pen *F* announcing my failures. He had only read one sentence of my paper. My philosophy in education centers on the idea of discipline. That's as far as he got. He never read the remaining six pages of philosophical point and counterpoint I had presented. The point of the entire class lesson that day was an hour long lecture on how I had gotten it all wrong. I didn't say a word as I sat quietly and tried to hide my embarrassment and then my anger for making me the laughing stock of the class. He had completely missed my point. He had used the wrong definition of discipline. Had he actually read my paper, he would have known what definition I was using. He was thinking of punishment. As the class drew to a close that morning I raised my hand. When called upon, I asked respectfully. "Sir you have clearly pointed out to us that we are not to punish our students, but definition number two in my dictionary says that discipline is regimen. Actually, it says, 'activity, exercise, or a regimen that develops or improves a skill; training,' and that's the definition I was using when I wrote my paper. Isn't that what education is when put into practice?"

He was caught off guard because He hadn't done his work. He dismissed the class and told me to see him in the hallway. As I exited the classroom the other students sat quietly waiting to hear what the outcome would be.

"You'd better have a good explanation for your outburst," he announced as the door shut behind me.

"I have a good explanation," I replied. "Actually, I have six pages of explanation," I handed him my paper. I explained how he had misinterpreted my work. I asked him to reread my paper. This time he took the time to read it. He had used a word incorrectly. He hadn't done the work he was supposed to do. He learned that day that words matter and how we use words and define them matters even more. I think that church people sometimes have the same problem as that professor. They don't understand the proper use of words.

It has been said many times that actions speak louder than words, but I have seen how the actions of others can send a message just as clearly as a text saying, "Don't invite Todd to the party."

Recently, I happened to attend the funeral of a distant acquaintance who had passed due to complications related alcohol abuse. As I sat in the funeral home, people filtered in. Two people stood out to me. One person was an individual with whom I had spent many hours as I earned my master's degree. To put it nicely, he was difficult to get along with. If we were assigned to a group project together, he wouldn't allow anyone else to give input. It was his way or the highway. The other person was someone I was familiar with socially before Sheryl became ill. We had mutual friends, and I had opportunities to get to know this individual. Sporting a bald head and long white bead, I tend to stand out in a crowd, and both of these people clearly saw me as they entered the funeral hall. Both clearly recognized me and decided to sit on the other side of the hall. As the service drew to a close, we were allowed to go forward to pay our last respects. Both of these individuals did exactly the same thing. Because they were seated closer to the front than I was, they went first. Each separately went forward to pay their last respects. Then they each turned around and viewed the crowd, made eye contact with me and then both could have exited down the center aisle and nodded to me as they passed within a few feet of me. Or they could have invested a few minutes and stayed around outside to visit with me. Instead, they each walked down the aisle as far from me as possible and were not around when I exited the hall. For whatever reason, neither of these individuals wanted to have any contact with me. As I climbed into my jeep that afternoon, I laughed quietly to myself. These two people nearly hurt themselves in avoiding me socially. I don't think either realized that I really didn't care if I talked with them or not. The easiest thing to do would have been to walk down the center aisle, nod to me as they passed, and then be on their way. Instead, they nearly ran over families on the far side of the hall trying to get away from me. A few years before, I would have been hurt. I would have wondered why they seemed to avoid me.

Caring for the Survivor

As I have moved past my past, set aside all the anger and bitterness, I don't let these types of interactions bother me anymore. It was clear to everyone at the funeral that these two individuals were acting differently from everyone else. They embarrassed themselves by acting differently. They didn't hurt me in any way because I don't look to them for approval. Ever since I unpacked all my emotional baggage alongside the road between Abilene, Texas and the Gulf Coast, I haven't gone back for it. I'm not going to let a couple of people I know from the community ruin my day.

As I worked through cancer with my wife and her subsequent death, my self-esteem took a big hit. The last year of her life, Sheryl made some very hurtful comments to me directly, comments I think were the result of the cancer moving into her brain. I also had people I thought were my friends who abandoned me and purposely chose to leave me out of their lives. I have had people that I knew from my church who were alone with just me in a hallway and chose to look away at a blank wall to avoid having to talk with me, and individuals at funerals avoid me at all costs. All of these actions from others eroded my self-esteem and self-confidence, but when I made the conscious decision to leave the hurt behind and not dwell on it, I began to gain self-confidence, and as I found success in tasks I was unfamiliar with, like cooking, I saw an increase in my self-esteem. My self-esteem had been tied to my perception of how others viewed me, not on my own views of my performance and skills. What's important to remember is that others are dealing with the very same struggles that I went through. So, when we are asking someone how they are doing, are we prepared to hear, "I'm struggling, I've lost my bearing," or "I don't have any reason to get up in the morning"? So, I have to ask, should we be caring for the survivor? Or does our care end when the loved one dies?

One of my biggest challenges has been the care and feeding of my son. It has also been the biggest reward. One of the self-help books I've read was "Resilience" by Eric Greitens 3. This book was the biggest help to me as I worked through the death of my wife. In this book, Greitens suggests that we need a reason for getting up in the morning, a reason for looking outside our grief and going through the motions of each day. He refers to "the reason" as *resilience*: a force that pulls us from our beds and gets us going each day. A reason for making sure the dishes are washed. A reason for staying plugged into life. A hobby, a practice of self-discipline, or a loved one. My resilience was my son. He had to be fed and cared for. He needed clean clothes to wear to school, good healthy meals, and a clean house. He needed someone to get him to practice and to cheer for him during sporting events. My son needed me to step up for his own mental health. I am not a person who makes giving

THE OTHER CANCER SURVIVOR

hugs a big priority, but I remembered from a college class that in a lab test, monkeys that didn't get hugs from their mothers would die from a lack of physical contact and caring. So, I made it a practice to be sure to give my son a hug every morning before he left for school. He would need the reaffirmation for his own development. This helped keep me moving forward each day as I sought to put my grief behind me. I needed to not let life hamstring me so my son could experience proper emotional growth.

As I stated earlier, I've been blessed to partner with others who are dealing with cancer in their lives, but my role, as I perceive it, hasn't been to care for the person with cancer, but the person who will survive the cancer, the spouse, child, or relative of the person who is dying. They need a resilient reason to get through each day, too. Sometimes it's simply a matter of "let's get a cup of coffee," but it gives that person a purpose for getting the day started, getting out of bed and, at the very least, going through the motions. Let me be real here: Some days, going through the motions is the best effort. It's far from ideal, but it's all the person has at that time to give that day. Do they care about the daily task at work? Do they care if the dishes get done? Do they care if the yard work is started? Nope! They realize that doing those tasks won't bring back the loved one. They realize that those tasks won't fill the void that's been left in their hearts, and they don't want to put forth the effort trying to overcome the difference. That's okay. As people work through the stages of grief and losing a loved one, it's okay not showing up for every day, but that's where I seem to fit in. My blessing is to help the survivor survive. I've had more than a few phone calls where the person calling is near to tears and can only yell and scream that life is unfair and that they feel like life has stacked the deck against them. I've been there, and I understand what they're going through, and I tell them that they are not alone in their feelings.

When my wife got cancer, her favorite color became breast cancer pink. I still have many things that are pink that she bought for me. Included on the list of my many pink things is a bright pink polo shirt. I also bought some pink canvas sneakers to wear to my wife's memorial service. When I'm answering the screaming phone calls or going to the hospital with a friend who's visiting a loved one dying from cancer, I get attached and emotionally involved, too. When that loved one dies from cancer, I make sure I wear my pink polo and shoes to work as a silent memorial to that loved one, but also to my new friend who's going through a tough time. I take a selfie and send it to them just to let them know that others care. Many times, I've had students ask me about why I'm wearing so much pink on a specific day, and I take a few moments to share about the person who just passed. One year in the course of six weeks I attended five funerals. My students got used to seeing me wear pink. One day I remember very well. A grandma had died from cancer, and I was wearing pink. As a student walked into my class, they looked at me and simply said, "Again?" "Yep sure enough," I replied. "I'm sorry. It sucks to be you," was the reply. Scripture says we are to bear one another's burdens. In society, we tend to care for the dying person easily, but I don't see as much care for the survivor. I'm blessed to get to be the one to care for the survivor. In many ways, it's become a second level of resilience for me.

Sheryl made me promise I'd wear a suit to her funeral. Here is the proof. Yes, those really are pink tennis shoes. Pink was the color of the day.

Soccer in suburbia. A very dangerous place for the unaccompanied Dad.

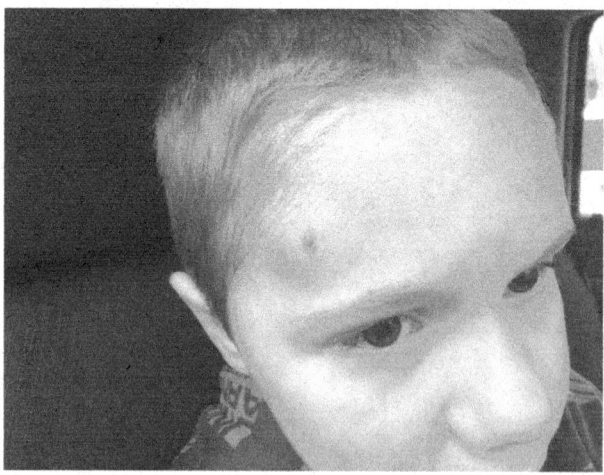

This what happens to the forehead when it makes contact with a metal tether ball pole at full kindergartener speed. That bump is quite literally the size of an egg.

Our "flat Stanley" green mustang that accompanied us over thousands of miles one summer as we traveled across the western U.S. When we returned, we were surprised to learn of the many who were following our travels via our online posts.

Now that it's just the two of us we make sure to get in many adventures. Hiking near San Diego.

The four corners of the U.S.

The great American experience of visiting Mt. Rushmore

Enjoying an afternoon at the ballpark in Salem Oregon.

Finding Normal

Normal?

NEVER IN A MILLION YEARS could I have imagined being where I am today. Of course people get old, and a spouse dies, but that's usually reserved for later in life like your seventies or eighties, not your forties. Being available to help others as they are forced to sit by and watch a loved one die was never on the list of occupations covered during career day in school. So, I find myself in a most unusual space: Others seek me out for help, assistance, guidance and informal grief counseling. These activities bring up memories that are usually too painful to talk about with others. No one wants to hear about the fear, loneliness, desolation, and emptiness associated with losing a loved one. No one wants to hear about the stab of grief deep within your soul because of a memory that is dragged to the front of your mind–until you are forced to go through it. The person in the middle of deep troubles finds comfort that they are not the only one to have those problems. I didn't have anyone to turn to for help. Nobody I knew had a spouse die from cancer. So, at times I pinch myself and wonder if I'm not living in a dream world. In fact, a recurring dream I have is waking up, and the entire cancer period of my life was just a dream. I wake up in my dream and go about my life only to wake up physically to the reality of my situation later. I've been asked why I didn't get counseling during this time. The simple answer is that I didn't have the time. I was already stuffing as much into a day as I could. I honestly didn't have time to sit down with a counselor and talk things over.

Nobody will ever accuse me of being a counselor, but in many ways that's the role I've taken on. My life is so completely different today than before, it would take pages to explain, but I can give just a few examples.

Before, I thought I had many friends. Now, I have very few friends, but as I help others walk through the death of a loved one, I make new friends who are bonded to me in a way that is closer than my closest friends from before. Cancer does that. Do I have the comfort of a spouse to come home to at the end of the day? Nope. But if I need help or if I need someone to scream at just because life has become too difficult, I have friends I can call. My life before Sheryl died was rich. I enjoyed amazing home cooked food, family outings, and time spent playing games with my son. Family time was plentiful and always an adventure. We enjoyed each other's company, and I spent time working a garden and caring for a house. Weekends were filled with fun family time. Now, I measure the fullness of my life based in part on how I am helping others. In many ways my life seems more spartan, but it's also richer. I don't get to play as many board games with my son as I used to. Instead, some of our father-son time is spent helping others, and that, as an act of resilience, has its own set of rich rewards.

My paradigm has changed so dramatically that the time before Sheryl's death seems a lifetime away, and in many ways it is. For the first time in my life, I cook my own food, and it usually tastes pretty good. I am self-sufficient. I care for my son and his needs along with myself. Nothing fancy, but the basics are covered. Before, I would glad-hand people and tell them I would be praying for their healing. I no longer pray for healing, but for comfort. I pray for deliverance from the pestilence and strength to endure the trial and for additional trust in God, but I chose my words carefully. I used to be so busy taking care of the necessary things in life that I didn't know anyone who was ill, nor did I have time to sit with others who were grieving. Now the grief-stricken seek me out. I make time to sit and relive my own experiences as a means of providing comfort to those in need.

Numbering Our Days

I used to expect I had decades left in my life. Now, I am more grateful for each new day. We don't know when our time here is done. No one really knows. Maybe six weeks before Sheryl got really sick and began her downward spiral, a lady in our community was headed to work. She was a teacher in town. It was her last day before maternity leave. A leave that would take her into the summer months. Her life was full, and her immediate future seemed to be planned. Her husband had left for work that day expecting he would return home, and that his wife and unborn child would be safe at home for months to come. No one expected the auto accident. No one expected having to bury not just a new mom, but a child, too. My first year as a teacher, I had a student in my economics class who failed miserably. I tried to get him interested in class, but he blew me off. He had more important things to worry about. He told me he'd make up the credit at an alternative school. Two months after our conversation, all he was doing that sunny spring day was standing at the bus stop. No one expected a drunk driver would swerve away from the bus and blow through the bus stop at two in the afternoon. No one expects that a simple check up at the doctor will reveal terminal cancer. Sheryl had undergone extensive testing just weeks before the tumors began to make her dizzy. By the time she was given the terminal diagnoses, we both felt a heaviness deep within our souls, but no one else expected such news.

We don't really know how long we have. At the same time, we cannot give up on life. We can't say life is worthless, there is no need to continue, and walk away from our responsibilities. It won't take long before we will need to pay the rent or buy food. Our loved ones will wonder what happened to us. Where did we go? The hardest part of life is living it. And let's be honest here, if I thought about all the dangers in life, I could wrap myself in bubble wrap and never leave my bedroom.

In 1948 C.S. Lewis wrote an essay about living in the nuclear age. Lewis postulates that nuclear war will occur, and that our end will come as a result of this type of conflict. At the time, Americans were digging bomb shelters in their backyards and preparing to survive nuclear winter. This existential threat was always present as I grew up—a child of the cold war. Each new day brought the possibility of dying like a flaming popsicle or going poof as our bodies exploded from the nuclear blast, but I was always raised to get the most out of every day. Checking out of life was never an option—an attitude that is in line with the thinking of Lewis. He states this theory on life as follows:

"If we are all going to be destroyed by an atomic bomb, let that bomb when it comes find us doing sensible and human things—praying, working, teaching, reading, listening to music, bathing the children, playing tennis, chatting to our friends over a pint and a game of darts—not huddled together like frightened sheep and thinking about bombs." 2

This also aligns with what the author Eric Greitens suggests. Find something that provides resilience 3. In other words, don't sit around soaking in your grief or worrying about tomorrow, but work on getting through today. If we are overwhelmed with events from life and death of a spouse, loss of a job, destruction of a business or property, then we need to find a person, activity, or pastime that will pull us through our remorse so we don't dwell on the severity of our situation. After the death of my wife, I was faced with a similar situation.

Living Life

As life happens, I find it odd how things time out. Sheryl died on her birthday exactly ninety days before Christmas. So, the year that she passed, I wasn't in the Christmas mood. I needed something to get my mind off of my troubles. As it would later prove to be my pattern, I took a road trip, but as always, there were people in my life who counseled me to not take the trip. Stay at home because travel in December is fraught with many dangers caused by winter weather. Or the alternate argument: There are many people on the open road who want to bring you harm, and you are putting yourself and your son in danger. I set aside their concerns and headed out. This time to Arizona for the wedding of a nephew. We had an enjoyable time and were able to get out of town and away from many memories. Because my son and I both operate on a school calendar, staying at home would have meant two weeks to sit and soak in our grief, something I didn't want to do. Five days on the road proved to be a greatly-needed break. The trip gave us a purpose. Were there risks? Yes. I had a couple thousand miles to have an equipment breakdown or get hit by another car. There were opportunities where someone could have attacked us as we walked into a store or restaurant. Yes, there were dangers, but those same dangers were waiting for us at home, and home offered many memories I didn't want to cope with. I know I didn't want to turn on the TV and see a favorite holiday movie and the associated memories. Cutting off my right arm with a dull implement would have been less painful. So yes, I avoided the pain, but if I was going to have a problem, then life would find me living life fully. That trip turned out to be a great start to many road trips throughout the following years.

Some people would say that travel with a young child can be a burden. I disagree. We waited many years to have a child, so our kid was really wanted. I was also prepared to deal with the added stress of daily activities with a kid. I'd like to point out that a child never needs a restroom until you're five hundred feet past the rest stop and the sign says next rest area sixty-five miles ahead, but traveling with a child in a camper that sits in a pickup bed is perfect. You just stop at the next exit where you get to use your own restroom. I also made it a practice that I would look for places to explore that were located about three hours travel time away from each other. So, in the morning we'd get moving and head out. Three hours later we'd arrive at a touristy place that would need to be explored. I looked for historical or cultural places to visit. Once we had exhausted the resources of the place we were visiting (on average 45 minutes) we'd move on. Lunch was eaten in the camper in either a church parking lot or a store parking lot, and then we'd repeat the process in the afternoon before making our way to our camping spot for the evening. I always stayed in an organized campground and would text a family member or a friend about where we were. Once we arrived at camp, if a pool was available, we'd get in a relaxing swim before dinner and table games in the evening. Earlier I stated that I didn't always have time to play games with my son. There were always too many things I needed to do to keep a house functioning, but on the road, in a camper, there was time.

I made it a habit to keep others informed of my whereabouts. My Dad was usually the person who was the base of contact on these trips. I'd text him and let him know when we left a campground in the morning, our expected route of travel, and our end destination for the day. Then throughout the day I'd let him know what was happening. And when we arrived at our camp-ground for the evening, I'd notify him that we'd arrived. If I didn't check-in, someone would eventually come looking for us. I also used Facebook to keep people updated. On one of our trips, we developed an informal following from each of our respective schools. Many people accompanied us virtually that summer.

Flat Stanley was a paper cutout person we used as a writing activity for elementary students. Students took Stanley with them and then wrote about his experiences. That summer, we modified the "Stanley." Instead of a flat piece of paper, "Stanley" was a green, Hot Wheels Ford Mustang, and we followed the same concept. The green "stang" visited Yellowstone and Dodge City and even made its way to the Gulf Coast and the Alamo in Texas. It also enjoyed many sights and sounds of Disneyland. With each entry in our travelogue, we'd include the front end of the "stang," "Stanley" was always present. That fall as we returned to school our colleagues helped us celebrate our summer with many conversations about our trip, but we wouldn't have had all of those memories if we hadn't taken the risk. If we'd had a problem on that trip, life would have found us celebrating our summer, not sitting at home lamenting our losses in life.

Life is full of dangers. I've been privileged to work in some production and construction jobs prior to being a teacher. I've watched fingers get removed from hands and arms get severely punctured from tools. I've had acid spilled on me and had chemical burns from exposure to toxic chemicals. I've seen others fall from equipment and break bones. I've been driving through town and seen vehicles collide with other vehicles. Accidents happen all the time, but we don't let that keep us from getting groceries or other home goods. My point here is that we live with the possibility of accidents and death every day, but usually, we survive. When we die, life will find us living life.

During the eighteen months between the end of treatment and the return of cancer, Sheryl made the unilateral decision that Saturdays were going to be family adventure days, and almost every Saturday involved some kind of family activity. We live in an area where it's an hour to the snow or an hour to the ocean and a river can be just a few minutes or a couple of hours away. A bike ride around a park is a common activity. The last good day that was spent at the baseball game is evidence of this mentality of life finding us living life. Cancer eventually caught up to Sheryl, but it had to hop into the back of my truck and hitch a ride to catch us long enough to make her dizzy. Only once it had taken hold did she give in to its demands and even then she was determined to beat it. When she was in the care home, she shunned visitors during the day time hours because she wanted to be rested for physical therapy. She understood that improved strength came from good rest and better therapy. One afternoon as I was visiting her room, she beamed with pride. She had succeeded at sitting in a wheelchair and kicking the balloon all the way down the hallway as a part of her physical therapy. She was determined to beat cancer. Only after she had lived out her calendar did she give up her will to live. I think that should be our attitude every day even if we don't have cancer.

My family knew a couple who conquered life every day. These dear people were in their eighties and retired, but their attitude toward life has always made me want to just keep on working. They were so busy in retirement that they didn't have time to let life get the better of them. The wife celebrated her eightieth birthday with a broken foot which she got from hiking on Mt. Rainier in Washington state. Travel was always the order of the day. Yes they took vacations but also traveled many miles with their trailer as a means of helping others in need. Carpentry tools were well worn from years of use. Life would find them living life. Even after years of cancer and many surgeries, the wife always had a smile on her face and was cheerful and happy to help others.

At the same time, I've had to work with people who are defeated just because the sun came up. Life is so difficult and such a trial. When you ask them what's defeating them that day, the response is, "Well...life is what's so hard."

This concept on how to live life is a conversation that I've had many times with people as they are in the mourning period after the death of a loved one. It usually takes three or four weeks, and then I'm approached with the question, how do you move on from something like this? My response is always the same: Embrace the pain fully and move on with little steps.

Handling the Pain

Facing the pain and confusion associated with the passing of a loved one is similar to addressing the needs of a cut to the hand. First, you want to stop the bleeding. I think this takes on the form of those afternoons when tears are just a breath away. You're fragile emotionally and may spend some time crying. That's okay. You'd do the same thing if you cut your hand. You'd scream as you reach for the cut to try and stop the flow of blood. Crying is a normal response to pain, but you still need to dress the wound. You treat the cut to kill bacteria. This might mean some rubbing alcohol or an antibacterial gel.

This means touching the cut. After the death of a loved one, we have much of the same thing to do. We need to set aside a few things for remembrance of a loved one but let other belongings go away. Engage the pain. Grab a hold of it and choke it until it no longer hurts. Yes, it hurts to let their belongings go away, but in the end you still have to deal with those belongings and let them go. If you wait, it just draws out the process and makes the pain last longer. The same holds true for the mental confusion that follows. I tried to fight it, and it got the better of me. Once I let go and let the confusion run my life, I soon began to function more fully. This will take weeks and months, but just go with it. Don't fight it. If you don't care for a wound to the hand, it will get infected and it will cause more pain. If you don't deal with the pain of losing a loved one, the loss can be a bigger issue if it isn't cared for early on. What follows with deep wounds are scars. These need attention. If you don't put some lotion on the scars regularly, they will catch on things like pockets, and you'll tear the scar open. So be careful and watch where you go and what you do, otherwise you'll end up in a situation that will cause deep memories to rise to the emotional surface and tear open your wounds. For me, the emotional lotion that I needed was a few minutes with my guitar each evening. Self-care is key. You've got to care for yourself and monitor where you are emotionally.

The practice began when Sheryl was enduring chemo treatment. She would get her dose of poison on Thursday mornings, and with one particular drug there was a lag time of about forty-eight hours before she would suffer from the effects. So on Saturday morning before she got sick, I would get us up and moving. We'd get a cup of coffee from our favorite coffee shack, and then we'd take a short drive in the countryside surrounding our city. An hour or so of meandering through farmland would refresh our souls. After she passed, and I needed daily informal counseling, it was time spent with my guitar, but Saturday morning usually found me meandering through nearby farmland taking a break from the stress of being alive. Both of these practices were easy ways for me to check out of reality for a few minutes and regain my emotional strength so I could navigate through life. When I talk with others, the question is almost always asked, "What should I do to relieve that stress?"

I answer the same every time: Anything that brings refreshment is the correct activity. Whatever brings peace is the correct activity. A hike, a run, or bike ride. Square dancing or quilting or needle point. Drawing or painting or carpentry. If it brings relief to your soul, then it is the right activity. Please note that drugs and alcohol will only mask the pain. They will only bring temporary relief. In the end, they will only hurt and not help, so I tell people to avoid these substances. Face your pain clean and sober, but remember that you don't have to deal with all of your grief in a single afternoon. Take it a little bit at a time and move on.

The key here is to move on. After the death of my wife, I heard about an individual who had also been living with the death of his wife. It had been seven years since she had passed, and he had yet to make any changes in his life. Her clothes were still in the dresser where she'd left them before her death. To me that seemed unusual. There is good mental health in moving on. I had time to prepare for my wife's death. So maybe two weeks after her passing I had family members over and let them divide up her belongings. I kept some for myself and my son as momentos for us. One thing I kept was a bracelet made of small stones. I had bought it for her as a gift. Another thing I kept was a special scarf with an animal print. It carried special memories for me. I did the same with my son. We looked at her things and he chose those items that carried the strongest memories of his mom. These things were set aside. We held the memorial service three and a half weeks after her passing, but her belongings were out of my house within two weeks. I was focused on moving on.

I don't remember anyone having this conversation with me. Maybe no one realized how much my life would change. Maybe they felt it was best if I just experienced it without being told, but I remember two pieces of advice I received. The first was that it would take a year before I really began to think clearly. They were right. It took me a year to the day before I began to see colors again. Thinking clearly took a little longer. The other piece of advice was that my friends would drift away. I understood that pretty fast, but if I were to have a chat with myself, I'd say that my life would never ever be the same, and that I needed to quit looking for the return to normalcy. Normal would take on a whole new meaning. It would be a night and day difference from my life before my wife got ill. Hang on. You're going to go through some serious changes and there is nothing you can do to stop it. So with that bit of information, I'd pat myself on the head and leave myself alone to ponder what the future held.

Normalcy? What exactly does that mean? I had a family member who would normally get food to fix for dinner on his way home from the store. A few weeks after his wife passed, he stopped as he normally did and was walking through the meat section trying to get his wife to answer the phone so he could ask her what she wanted for dinner. Normalcy? I always got my wife special chocolates to celebrate special dates. I was standing in line at the chocolate store that first Christmas season when it registered in my mind that I no longer needed to get her chocolates. She wouldn't be eating these candies. Normalcy? I always had my wife help me choose which tie to wear. She did a much better job at selection than I ever would. Now that she has passed, I usually don't wear a tie. Usually, you come home from work and the person is at home waiting for you. When they aren't present is when the pain starts. Change in the normal is the cause of the emotional pain. Before Sheryl got sick, I planted and cared for a garden. A change from the normal meant I didn't care for a garden and seeing the empty plot of land caused emotional pain. Normalcy is where we find comfort. Not having normalcy can be stressful.

Moving Beyond Normal

I was in college and the class was westward expansion. The course of study explored what caused us as a people to move across the continent and the cost that we paid as a nation to make that move. I gained much knowledge from that class, and not all of that knowledge was in history. One thing I observed was how we as humans operate in a state of normalcy and how being outside that state can cause severe stress.

The assignment given on day one was to research a person of historical significance to our class and prepare a five minute oral presentation to present to the class. There were about forty-five of us in class and, as chance would have it, I was in the slot numbered somewhere around thirty. We were to keep track of each presenter and their historical figure and turn in our log at the end of the term. I watched again and again as every presenter slowly made their way to the front of the class and began with a monotone voice, "I did my historical person on..." They would state who they were presenting, and the class would write down the name of the historical person and promptly perform a mental check out for the next five minutes. This practice bothered me quickly. How boring. How mundane. How normal.

Then it was my turn. If I was going to go to the effort of researching a person and presenting, I wanted people to pay attention to what I was saying. It was time to move away from normal. The professor called on me to present. I stood to my feet. "Today I want to tell you about the individual who is credited with first dreaming of the idea of a rail line that would stretch from the Atlantic Ocean to the Pacific." I then stepped away from my desk and continued, "The idea of a transcontinental rail line was first proposed in 1839, before the era of the rotating wheel assembly." I had made it to the aisle and began to move towards the front of the room. I continued telling the class all about my historical person, and I had them eating out of my hand, hanging on every word. Pencils ever so delicately poised over their historical persons log waiting for me to tell them whose name they were to write down. I continued giving detail after detail until I was interrupted by the professor.

"I didn't hear who you were presenting on."

"Yes", I replied, "I haven't told you yet."

A peer chimed in, "The suspense is killin' me." I continued to expound demonstrating learned knowledge of this person and his accomplishments and explaining in great detail how he had impacted expansion as a nation westward. I had reached the point in my presentation for the dismount. Every single person to this point had finished with something like "that's all I have" or "that's it." I saved the most important information until the very last.

"My person of historical significance is William Redfield." An audible sigh filled the room as my classmates hurriedly scribbled down the name I had given them before sinking into their desks. The stress had been lifted. Every person had paid attention to every word I had spoken because I gave them a reason to listen. I didn't spoil the end. It wasn't the usual. It was different. It was unique in that every person that followed me went right back to the same monotone delivery that had preceded my presentation. As a class, we returned to "normal," and I sat in the back of the room silently dying from boredom.

What if normal isn't really good for us? What if normal needs to be torn down and rebuilt? Is that what happens when a married couple gets a divorce because they've seemed to have grown apart? Why did they grow apart? Was the normal boring and they went looking for something new and interesting? And as they looked for something different, they went in different directions? Why do we change hobbies? Why do we seek out different careers? Why do we try out a new restaurant?

What are trials really? From the Judeo/Christian perspective they are the work of an Almighty Creator improving us spiritually, but it isn't fun. It is a challenge. It hurts. It causes pain and discomfort. Through trials we grow in faith, but from a non-faith based perspective, they are merely coincidence, a combination of forces directing change in our lives. A young driver gets a flat tire in the middle of rush hour and has to change the tire on the side of the road. All the while, cars are whizzing by and honking horns at the teen because the flat tire caused a back-up slowing the flow of traffic. It's a difficult situation, but if the young driver learns from the trial, he will make sure that his tires are properly inflated, and he will avoid sharp objects in the road, a lesson that is easily learned.

Some trials don't readily reveal what the lesson should be or what learning took place. How can we quantify change? I had a really good life. I was blessed in many ways. Now that I've lived through the death of my spouse, my life has undergone changes that were 180 degrees opposite from the life I had been living. I don't know how the two different lives can be compared.

If Sheryl hadn't gotten cancer and passed away, my life would have been fulfilled. I was achieving my goals. Vacations would have been limited to a couple weeks in the summer and a couple weekends each year. I wouldn't have had the many opportunities to spend six or eight weeks traveling across the Western United States. I was content to let Sheryl do the cooking. She was a great cook. When I'm cooking, it's an adventure. You never know what's gonna catch fire or get burnt. Maybe the chicken will be heated enough not to make us sick. Is your insurance paid up?

Life was good, but it was routine and comfortable. It was normal. Since Sheryl passed, my normal has been anything but normal. A few years ago, a single mom friend of mine was having some behavioral problems with her daughter. Nothing serious was happening, just a few simple tantrums and crying for unspecified reasons, but concerns were voiced and questions raised. After a couple of counseling sessions it was suggested by the counselor that a backwards night might be a nice treatment alternative. The thought was that the daughter was used to things happening a specific way each day, and when that didn't happen, she would throw a tantrum. Backwards night was designed to change the expectations. It was presented as a fun-filled alternative adventure. Step one, get into pajamas. After all, what's the last thing you do before you go to bed? Jammies and pink fuzzy bunny slippers. Step two, the pre bedtime story and on and on until the evening has been completed from end to start. Dinner began with dessert and was eaten with the plates and glasses placed on the floor and not the table. The last half hour before they actually went to bed, they changed back into street clothes and ended the evening fully dressed ready to walk out the door. It worked. The daughter quit expecting certain things to happen at specific times, and their lives smoothed out.

As I take a giant step away from my circumstances, I can see that the five months that I cared for Sheryl was like a giant, elongated, backwards night. My life was so completely different from a normal life that it's hard to explain. I didn't clean the house. I didn't fold the laundry. I washed my clothes but I was in such a rush to care for my wife and so overwhelmed by life's events that I piled it on the couch and left it there for days on end. A dear friend who had a key to my house was dropping off some food for our meals and spent an hour folding my clothes for me. Life was out of control. It was a supersized reset on my life.

After Sheryl passed, I had to settle into the new normal. If I had attended a counseling session or had any formal group therapy, I might have been told that the old normal was gone, and I would need to create a new normal, but isn't that why trials come? Their purpose in our lives is to cause us to take a step backwards and reexamine how we live. The hard times provide a reason to examine what we do, and why we do what we do, when we do those things we do.

In America, we have so many of our needs met that we expect things to just be present all the time. When they aren't present we get upset. We get angry. Recently my community went through an ice storm. Freezing rain left an inch of ice on everything. Trees and power lines failed under the added weight of the ice. I went four days without power and everything in my home is powered from electricity. It was cold outside and cold inside. I would sit on the couch staring at the wall and wearing three layers of clothes and a blanket over my shoulders to try and stay warm. When it got dark out we had to use flashlights to be able to see. I went to bed early because it meant that I could climb into my sleeping bag and get warm. Out of routine, I would enter a room and flip on the light switch. I was always surprised when the lights didn't turn on. I had to eat out because I couldn't power the stove to cook any food. When I returned home I would walk through my front door expecting a wave of heat to greet me. I was surprised when it was colder inside than out. A few days after the power was restored, the weather forecast called for more snow. I momentarily panicked because I didn't want to relive the experiences of the previous week.

I classify this as a trial. As a result of this storm, portions of society broke. Normally it takes fifteen to twenty minutes to order take-out pizza. It seemed like half of society ordered pizza on the first night of the ice. I had to wait almost two hours for my pizza to get cooked. One customer had called hours before with a large fourteen pizza order and it was never made. He never got his pizza that evening. Grocery stores already suffering supply issues due to covid restrictions ran out of goods and had empty shelves. Because of downed trees, roads remained closed for weeks. I understand that for some parts of the world this is normal. They don't have the infrastructure to support a bustling society. Shortages and power outages are common. I've never been through a hurricane. I live where I live so I don't have to go through a hurricane. I'm going to make a guess and say that if you're a hurricane veteran it's not that bad, but for me, it would be traumatic because I've never done it before. I would need to broaden my experience to better understand hurricane preparedness, just like that lifelong citizen of southern Florida who's never experienced an ice storm. If they were to wake up one winter's day to an inch of ice all over South Florida, they would be traumatized. They live where they live so they don't have to endure the cold icy winter weather. They would see society fail, too.

Why was the ice storm such a big deal? Because expectations weren't being met. I didn't throw a fit and cry, but I did make a mental note to get better prepared. I had switched domiciles the previous month and had yet to set in place stop gap measures to use in case of a catastrophe, like an ice storm. I have learned through other experiences to be prepared. The same thing happens when a loved one gets cancer. Expectations aren't being met. We have events planned on our calendars for weeks and months in advance. We have annual plans, like a super bowl party, and family events like anniversaries and annual camping trips. We wake up each day expecting to attend those events. When a loved one gets terminal cancer all of those events come to a screeching halt. Immediately! I expected the day would eventually come when one of us would pass. I just wasn't expecting it to happen in our forties. People get sick all the time. People die for many reasons, but the change in paradigm caught me off guard. I needed to adjust. I was stressed because my expectations weren't being met. In the years since the death of my wife, new normal has been established in my life.

Long Term

Care for the Living

Earlier I shared about caring for the survivor, that person who's left picking up the pieces of what's left of life, the person who needs care and assistance and attention, the person who's been invisible for days or weeks or even months as visitors hurried by to spend time with the terminally-ill loved one, the person who's trying to establish some semblance of order and normalcy. So, what does that actually look like? How do we care for the living?

First of all, acknowledge that they aren't the person who died. They are still upright and taking nourishment. They have needs and wants and still enjoy time with friends. In my case, I wanted to get a cup of coffee with a friend and see what was happening in his life. I had spent five months checked out of the normal day-to-day routine of life while caring for my wife. High school graduations had happened and grandchildren had been born. People I knew had gotten married and another set of friends had divorced. Seasons had gone from spring through summer and into fall. I missed my summer vacation and all the pictures from other people's travels.

Through the last couple of weeks of my wife's life, people went past me as they made their way into see my wife. I was just the person who answered the door and picked up toys in the front room. The day my wife died was the lone exception. My closest friend took my phone and told me he was going to be the gatekeeper for the day. Nobody had direct contact with me via my phone, and if I was approached physically, he was present. Always ready to assist in any way. As the afternoon progressed, it was determined that people needed to move their cars so the mortuary could get access to my property. He asked individuals to move their cars. I simply sat and absorbed the changes in life. For the next couple of days, I was cared for and was driven where I needed to go so I would be able to spend my efforts on grief and not navigating traffic. I was cared for.

Tailgating

I began many pages ago with the notion that my friends would drift away, and they did. Things would progress to no one asking how I was or what was happening in my life. But in the first couple of months after Sheryl died, I was still checked on occasionally and people demonstrated to me how special I was to them through their actions.

Just a couple of weeks after I returned to work, a coworker demonstrated through her actions just how much she really cared about me. I was teaching a class when a student I didn't recognize walked in and handed me an envelope with my name on it. Inside was a card signed by a number of students and other staff members. Included was a Starbucks card and a set of instructions. Being a graduate of Oregon State University, I thoroughly enjoy attending any game where the Beavers were participating. My coworker knew this, so in cooperation with other staff members, they used their contacts at the University to secure for me a pair of tickets for that week's football game. I asked my coworker if she could accompany me to the game, but she had other plans, so I invited yet another coworker to the game and knew we would have a most excellent time. I expected these seats to be located near the top of the stadium and have a limited view of the field. I was shocked to learn that I would need special access to the section of the stadium and booster club where the seats were. It was a cold and foggy night in November, and temps hovered in the upper thirties except where we sat—under cover where heaters kept the ambient air temp in the low fifties. I shed my heavy coat as we settled in for the game. In the end, the Beavers got destroyed and lost the game by almost fifty points. I didn't care. Because of the pregame tailgate with other teachers from my school and the late hour of the game, I was able to spend many hours just being a person at a college football game. When the tailgate began pregame, there were comforting words that passed between us as the food was being heated, and then the conversation found its way to other topics. After the game, the tailgaters that we gathered with were settling in for the second round of food and desserts. I needed to get home and return to my duties. We said our goodbyes, and I headed for home. As I view this day through the lens of many years, I realize that together we had moved on and past the events of the previous seven months. In the weeks and months that followed, as I passed these other "tailgate" teachers in the hallway at school, our relationship as co-workers continued to grow. It wasn't restricted because words and topics weren't addressed. I will always be grateful for my friends and coworkers who cared enough to get me away from my troubles for a few hours. It was a special time that I can't recreate.

Movie Night

The following week, we had some snow, and school was canceled. Another set of friends decided to have a movie night, and we were invited. I was told that I didn't need to bring anything, just show up. We enjoyed a warm potluck and rich conversation with much laughter. No one was in a hurry to start the movie, and time was passing. My schedule meant that we were up at 5:30 each morning. On days that we didn't have school, my son was still up early because he was used to the early mornings. I had also learned that if I kept him up late he was still up early and then had troubles with emotional outbursts the next couple of days. I needed him to be mellow and relaxed as much as possible because that made my troubled days that much smoother.

So, as friends began to gather and settle in for the movie, I began the process of leaving the party. That meant bundling up my son and getting his shoes on and finding where my coat was. Everyone looked at me funny as I opened the door to leave. In fact, the host sat on the couch and said, "Well, ah, see ya later."

Time would pass, and many months later after everyone had quit talking to me, I was approached by an acquaintance and asked why I was so angry with people. I asked for clarification. My actions as related to this party were pointed out as being the origin of the opinion that I was angry. The truth was that I wasn't angry with anyone. I was lonely. I had been trying to get a cup of coffee with any friend that would get together with me. I was struggling to find a footing in life, but I wasn't angry. No one had asked why I left early. It was just assumed that I was mad about something. If I was angry, it was because I didn't have any choice as I saw it but to get home and keep my kid on a regular schedule. A movie would have been enjoyable, but I didn't have time to watch a movie, I had to deal with life.

ASK!

If someone had asked what was going on, I could have told them about my need to get my son to bed at a regular time. I would have volunteered to call them first thing in the morning so they understood what time I really got up. I would have taken the time to explain my struggles with my calendar and that I really didn't have any extra time in a day and that the four hours I'd already spent at the movie night dinner party had actually set me behind two days on my list of chores. But nobody asked, they just got offended. So many things affect our daily schedules, and getting to bed is an important part of scheduling our day. I wanted to be sure I didn't set my son up for failure by keeping him up late and on an irregular schedule. He was already stressed enough as it was. I know I was having a hard time making the adjustment to single dad life, and my son would have given anything to get a hug from the mom he missed. Again, no one asked.

The same has been true for other social gatherings. I have avoided Valentine's Day since the day my wife passed, but every year, I get invited to a Valentine's dinner. So ask yourself, why would I enjoy being the only single person, with a bunch of married couples who are really only interested in spending time with each other on this particular night? If I don't attend, I'm not upset. I'm just avoiding a difficult social situation.

The reason I keep getting asked to Valentine's dinner is because no one has taken the time to think through the situation. I understand they are being kind and trying to involve me, but this may not be the best solution. It is simply assumed that I want to be at a Valentine's dinner without a Valentine, and no one took the time to ask why I was leaving the movie night early. It was just assumed that I was angry about something. Those people who had been supporting me and my wife while she was sick had quit asking me questions about me. When she was sick there was a meal train set up, and I didn't need to do anything for my evening meal except coordinate the delivery. No one needed to ask me any questions about likes or dislikes or allergies because that was all covered on the meal train web site. So by the time I was single, there was no need to ask my opinion. No one checked in on me, and I was generally left on my own. When I left the movie night, the same thing happened. Assumptions were made, and I was assigned the emotion of being angry.

Someone to Talk To

I would talk with my friends and many of them would say something to the effect of "Anything I can do to help, just let me know." So often I'd respond with the suggestion of getting a cup of coffee. I will admit that I love coffee. Black. Straight with no froo-froo stuff added. Don't give me a straw. That'll just slow me down, and yes, leave the pot or thermos or carafe, and yes, I'll be happy to get one to go. Just get it brewing or pull the shots of espresso. Either way, I would really appreciate a cup of coffee. Only one person took me up on the invite, and that was limited to only a couple of times. I understand that people are busy and that many people had taken time out of their busy lives to help me care for my wife. Prior to my wife getting ill, I could always find someone to join me for coffee. So what changed?

I think what changed was that those who were my coffee connections were afraid to talk to me about events in life. I didn't care if we talked about my life or theirs. I just wanted someone to talk to. I wanted to see how their favorite team was doing. Choose a sport and let's talk about it. Are they thinking about buying a new car? Making improvements to the existing one? Did they decide to add wallpaper to the wall that they can't decide what to do with in the living room? Any topic was an appropriate topic to talk about. We didn't have to talk about Sheryl and her illness and passing. In fact at this point in my life, the topic of her passing had kind of worn thin for me. I was over it and making changes in my life and wanted to leave my past behind me. I wanted to get on with life. I didn't want to dwell in the past. I didn't care if we talked about me or them or the weather. I just wanted someone to talk to just like we had done before. Nobody wanted any coffee.

What I have observed is that people don't know what to say to the survivor. People don't want to inflict additional pain, and I understand that. So instead of saying something wrong, possibly offending the survivor, they just don't say anything at all. The key word here is survivor. The not-dead person. The person who's still upright and taking nourishment. Breathing. Trying their best to live life as full as they can and are weighed down by the recent passing of a loved one. In the months that followed my wife's passing, I would joke about death or dying. Surprised that I would be joking about such a topic, people would get offended. Why they got offended I don't know because they weren't the one who was still trying to recover from the loss of a loved one. I was. I am the survivor. We need to acknowledge that an event has happened and move on. Getting a cup of coffee with a friend is a great opportunity to make that acknowledgement and have the opportunity to reconnect with the person.

Let me put this another way. Would people ignore me if I were in a horrible car accident and lost my legs as a result? And having spent months in recovery, was now trying to get back to work and find life's new normal? Or if we actually did go out for a cup of coffee, would the friend acknowledge the fact that I was now in a wheelchair? Would they ask me about challenges I was facing? Maybe? Or maybe not. It is through these types of difficult challenges that a person finds out who their real friends are and who is faking the whole friendship thing.

So, what is the difference between the movie night and football game? Both were special events, and I was invited to each by friends that cared enough to demonstrate for me in real physical actions that they cared. In both cases, I attended for as long as I could. Time and the ticking clock were always a thought that was present in the back of my mind. The difference between both events was the response to my needing to exit the activities. I was allowed to leave the football game gathering and not participate in the post-game tailgate. No one was upset, but others couldn't understand why I would leave a movie night and not watch the movie. Also included in the mix was a sitter for my son. I didn't have a sitter available the night of the movie. I would need to get home early and get him to bed, but for the football game, I was able to get a sitter for my son, so he was in bed by half time.

Two Divergent Dinners

I heard a car in the driveway but couldn't get to the door before they rang the bell. Friends who had signed up on our meal train were delivering our evening meal. Both husband and wife were available to visit and we were glad to see them. As they entered our home, I realized that they were bringing more than just a meal. Yes, they had a large cardboard box full of still warm culinary delights, but they also brought encouragement. Included in our meal delivery this evening was a personalized card with messages of care and love and a medium sized bouquet of fresh flowers. The card would spend the next couple of weeks within arm's reach of where my wife had established her life, and the flowers would sit within eyesight so she could enjoy their beauty. Once the parcels were placed in the fridge or set in place around our front room, these friends sat down and checked in on us. They asked probing questions of how well we were coping and dealing with cancer, and how well I was doing with the changes in life. Did I need help with the yard? These were friends that knew how to show that they cared.

Fast forwarded a few weeks later. The doorbell rang and this time, before I could once again get to the door, dinner was placed on our front step and the lady was walking back towards her car. "Hey, how ya doin'?" I greeted.

"I really don't have time to visit. I am running errands and thought I'd drop your dinner off on the way. Oh, and you might want to refrigerate the chicken. I don't know how long it was sitting on display at the grocery store, and then it sat in the car for a while cause I made a couple of stops along the way. Anyway I gotta go. Bye."

I didn't even have a chance to get a word in, and she was back in her van and pulling onto the street. As I closed the door, my wife stated matter-of-factly, "Well, I guess it was nice of her to care enough to bring dinner." I went into the kitchen and promptly threw the entire chicken into the trash. I didn't want dinner to make me sick. Later I made up some leftover potato soup for my wife. My son and I had pizza.

I want to be fair and say that not everyone has time to make a home-made meal every day, and not everyone has time to get flowers and a card and spend time asking real questions. But these two divergent dinners are a prime example of people caring for others.

It's okay to just get a cup of coffee and have a conversation and not make a big deal about it, much like the chicken that was left on my front porch. We need those every day, run-of-the-mill activities. Without them, the exceptional becomes the norm, but the other meal with flowers and a card was a special gift. There is nothing wrong with something special. If you're going to do something special for the survivor, then make it super special and elevate your expectations. Make it bigger than what you'd normally do. Then, if you can, accompany the survivor to that activity. Yes, make them feel special, but offer the extra special super extravaganza part by being in the event, like enjoying special seats at a football game with them.

Caring for the surviving person can be a challenge because their life is in an uproar. Their paradigm has shifted and they are trying to understand where the new norm lies, but by attending the special event with them or getting a simple cup of coffee, you help to smooth out the bumps in the new road. It's easy to care for the dying person. They have a limited amount of time, but for the survivor, the care team might have to be on duty for many years. It is the care for the survivor that really matters because they are the person that will breathe life back into our relationships. Yes, we lose when a person dies, but we shouldn't lose both people, and not caring for the survivor is like those empty phrases that are offered when a person is dying. Emptiness. If we say we really care about someone, if we speak words to encourage others, then our actions should speak louder than our words.

Unexpected Twist

My Turn

I had been having trouble swallowing, and someone told me they noticed that I was continuously clearing my throat. Red flags began to wave madly in my mind. Let me explain: When I was in the military, I was directly in the path of the fallout during the Chernobyl melt down. Western Europe wasn't supposed to be greatly affected, we were told, but as time has progressed, I've come to disagree. A main cause of thyroid cancer is exposure to higher levels of radiation. That is the only time that I know of that I was expose to radiation. Throughout the years, I've worked in many different construction, deconstruction, and production jobs. I know I've inhaled asbestos and old powdery lead-based paint. I have had acid spilled on me and been exposed to so many toxic chemicals to the point that one spring I broke out in a nasty, itchy, scaly rash. Big angry red blotches covered my body, and I was scratching them till I bled trying to get in to see someone from the medical community. After a brief examination, I was given a chemical burn cream to apply topically and an oral medication that dialed back my immune system, which was working overtime and literally eating my body. In short, I've been exposed to many chemicals, and any one of them could cause cancer. Difficulty swallowing scared me.

I made my appointment and waited the six weeks to get to see my doctor. Because it is clearly stated in the Hippocratic Oath that a doctor check the patient's throat whenever they are seen, he felt the need to look in the back of my throat, and I was diagnosed with acid reflux. Nothing to worry about, he reassured, and I was prescribed a super powerful version of an over-the-counter medication and charged a heavy fee. I didn't have any problems with acid indigestion or other warning signs of acid reflux. I pressed my point and explained to him my history around cancer-causing chemicals, and that if the proper tests were conducted, the government would probably label me a chemical waste dump, and I would only be allowed to be cremated in specific mortuaries that had the chemical scrubbers in place to protect the environment. He thought for a moment and scratching his chin replied, "Well, before we can do anything or refer you to a specialist, we are required to conduct blood tests for six months unless a test has results that determine you have cancer, which at that point, you'd be referred."

"What kind of tests are we talking about?"

"Oh, just a simple blood test. It's not that big a deal really. How do you feel about getting a blood test?"

I agreed to the test on the spot and made my way to the lab for the test before heading home. Now the waiting began. I had been here before with Sheryl. I was to go home and sit quietly, and if it was really bad, I'd get a call. I had seen how that turned out. I nervously waited for a call. When the results came back, they were out of whack. The doctors didn't think I had cancer but weren't sure what was going on. I began a six-month period of blood tests every two weeks as my results were plotted on a graph. The first test showed I lacked thyroid stimulating hormone. The next time my numbers were high. Big swings in my blood results were causing my team of doctors to question what was really happening. I was confused, a little scared, and at the mercy of the medical community which, at the time, wasn't sharing any information with me.

Did I say that?

Weeks after my initial visit with my doctor I happened to be at the dentist. All of my medical and dental needs were covered by the same provider, so my dentist had all of my medical information. As my dental visit wound down, and my new crown was securely in place, my very caring dentist told me he was sorry that I had cancer but that he was pulling for me and wished me the best of luck during my treatments. The look of surprise was enough to startle him. He looked me square in the eye and stated, "I don't think you've been told you have cancer yet, have you?" I reassured him that I was grateful for his honesty and thanked him for his services. As I drove home, I pondered how I was going to break the news to my son. The thought, "Your mom died from cancer four years ago, and if things don't go right, you could be an orphan" kept repeating itself in my mind, but I didn't have any information on which to base my explanation.

I needed to wait another two weeks for the official notification from a medical doctor, and then he wasn't sure I needed to have surgery. I stopped him mid-explanation, and as politely as I could without being offensive, informed him that I needed a doctor that was going to be as aggressive and tenacious as an angry wolverine in treating my disease. I had a young son who needed a parent, and if he felt like he couldn't be aggressive towards my treatment, then would he please refer me to someone who would. He assured me he would be gung-ho towards getting me better, and we agreed on surgery.

As I prepared for surgery, I needed to have a talk with my son. I wanted to be sure he didn't panic when he heard the word "cancer" being spoken. I explained to him that some cancers were more deadly or aggressive than others. We talked about skin cancer, and that if it is caught early, a spot on the skin is removed, and then you don't have cancer anymore, and you live a long and healthy life. I reassured him that not everyone who has cancer dies from cancer. I then told him that I had a weak and slow-moving form of cancer that probably wouldn't kill me if I got the cancer treated. After a

10-15 minute conversation about cancer, he said he understood what was going on and that he wasn't scared of the outcome.

Since my wife passed away, I've made two friends who have also lost loved ones to cancer. They are my friends and fill a void in my life but also serve as an informal cancer survivor's group. These two dear friends informed me that on my surgery day, they would get me to the hospital and home again the next day. I checked into the hospital for surgery. My day for surgery was Thursday. I liked this because I could be back home by the weekend. My only complaint was that the drugs they were giving me for post procedural pain left me feeling very brittle and caused me to see everything in various shades of shadow. It wasn't frightening but left me feeling unsettled. After surgery I usually feel like I have the flu and have been in a car accident all at the same time. Sleep and time spent on the couch are the best cure for these side effects. Only this time, I wasn't given a chance to recover. I had to step up and care for Tucker. I was given adult supervision, but by evening of the first day home, I was all alone. Day number two I went about my usual routine, got groceries, and did my running around. On day number three after surgery, I was trying to relax but kept needing to do things that placed stress on my upper body, things like doing the laundry. I didn't have a choice. It had to get done, and I was the only one available to do it. I lifted and carried loads of dirty laundry to the clothes washer. Once they were dry, I carried them to the bedroom where I folded them and put them away. I didn't think there would be any repercussions, and as I went to bed that night I slept peacefully, but in the back of my mind, I felt a need to lay face down. Something didn't feel right in my neck.

When Procedures Go Bad

The next day was Monday, and I got Tucker to school before returning home to continue my recovery. I refilled my cup of coffee and sat down to watch some television, but I was once again having difficulty swallowing. I went into the bathroom to see if I could see if I was having troubles with the incision. The incision was fine. No sign of infection. From my vantage point looking directly at myself in the mirror, everything looked a little swollen, so I sent myself to the urgent care clinic. Something just wasn't right.

When I got to the clinic, they took one look at me and immediately called an ambulance, and I was taken to the emergency room at the local hospital. As I was wheeled into the ER, a nurse started in with the usual questions: name, date of birth, blood type, what was the cause of my vis—

She stopped mid-question and looked at me for the first time. The look on her face told me that I was in serious trouble. She began to shout out instructions calling for IVs and a doctor, blood work, and for imaging to prepare for an emergency scan.

I had called my sister-in-law and asked her to come to the ER and to notify the rest of the family. Things had gotten serious, and I was going to need help. She quickly arrived at the hospital and decisions were discussed. The doctor told me I was going be intubated but not to worry because I would be unconscious, and that I wouldn't feel a thing. I didn't have a chance to get excited or worry because about that time, a nurse put a drug into my IV, and I was out.

I only know what took place over the next four days because of what I've been told. The doctors in the emergency room had difficulty getting a tube down my throat. As they were struggling to get me tubed, a serious discussion was held regarding my need for a tracheotomy, and a surgeon began scrubbing and prepping for the procedure in case ER staff couldn't get a tube inserted. In the end, I was tubed with a child-sized tube because an adult-sized tube was too big. The argument could be made that I'd waited too long to seek medical attention. Later, after I got out of the hospital, I was told to not ever wait as long as I did. Apparently, things were very close to reaching a catastrophic level. I fought with staff and tried to take out my tube because my arms were tied to the bed when I came to. One of the bruises didn't even make a showing until I'd been home for a week. Someone really had to sit on me to get me to behave. I was also transferred from the hospital in Salem to a larger hospital in Portland. All this excitement, and I missed it all.

When I was brought out of the medically-induced coma, I was in a fog and was having trouble clearing my head. I soon realized that I had something stuffed down my throat, and I couldn't reach it because my arms were strapped to the bed rails. Then nurses and my brother began asking me questions, not simple yes and no questions, but questions that required a more complex answer than just shaking my head. My brother, who was present, began to laugh. He thought this was really funny. He took great joy in watching me try to figure it all out. This also explains why Mom and Dad had me first because I'm so much more likeable than he is. It was probably only a few seconds, but it seemed like an eternity when he suggested they get me some paper and a writing utensil so I could answer their questions. My arms were untied only after I promised not to remove the tube myself. For the remainder of the day, the questions came, and those in my room waited patiently while I scribbled down my answers.

A Breath of Air

Good news, I was told. The swelling had gone down, and the tube was to be removed, but they also wanted to run a couple of tests first to be sure I didn't have any problems from when they tubed me. Okay, I thought, let's get the tests done. I don't know if I ever understood what the delay was, but it took a couple hours before the tests were conducted. It may have been an issue of assembling all the staff. It may have been a need to get me more fully conscious. Regardless, it was a very long couple of hours. As I regained more awareness, I became more conscious of the tube extending deep into my throat. Anytime it touched the side of my throat, I'd gag. At any other time, I'd laugh about gagging and move on, but I was still attached to the machine on the other end of the tube in my throat, and when I gagged, the tube end would fill up with lung butter. This was bad. When the tube filled with mucus, I couldn't breathe. I couldn't get air out, and I couldn't get air in. My lifeline, who was a very attentive nurse, would then put a solid plunger down the breathing tube and clear out the obstruction. This happened more times that I wanted to count. At one point, I looked across the ICU at my brother as I lay in the bed trying not to gag, and he looked at me and straight faced said, "Don't gag." That's all it took. Just a simple suggestion. I gagged so hard my entire body jerked in one giant convulsion, and the tube filled up with lung butter. I fought to exhale so I could get fresh air into my lungs. The machine began to beep its alarm. The nurse plunged the tube clearing the airway, and I was able to exhale, but when she pulled the plunger out a suction was created and the tube filled once again. Only now I couldn't get air in. She plunged again, and I was able to breathe through my small, child-sized breathing tube. While all this was going on, I was watching a clock on the far wall trying to keep myself from panicking. The realization that a cold sweat had broken out on my forehead entered my brain. I watched as forty-five seconds ticked away while I struggled with the help of my nurse to get a clear airway. I struggled against shear panic and terror and tried not to let it overtake me that afternoon. Thoughts of water boarding entered my mind. Oh but wait, more fun was still to come.

As my bed was wheeled into the surgery suite, a team of doctors and specialists had assembled, and I felt a little self-conscience as fifteen people in all were watching my every move. The surgeon explained what tests needed to be completed before they could remove the tube and that they needed to numb up my throat and lungs. Levers were flipped and buttons pushed and my restriction to breathing only through the tube was lifted. Liquid was poured down my breathing tube, and it splashed into my lungs, and I coughed it out just like I was instructed to. Only now I couldn't breathe. I began to gasp for air. I couldn't tell if I was getting any air into my lungs, and I was panicked. I gulped air like a man trying not to drown. A hand on my shoulder belonging to a male voice told me that my blood oxygen levels were near one hundred percent. I was getting air I just couldn't feel it. I just needed to breathe normally. It took a couple of moments before I began to regain some semblance of normal breathing. Next was a visual exam of my throat and vocal cords via my nose, and then the tube was removed. The surgeon promptly asked me how I was feeling. I replied as calmly as I could. "That things sucks! Who wants to go next?" A doctor who was within arm's reach immediately took three giant steps backwards. I so wanted to look at him and say, you didn't ask mother may I, but I let it slide. "Is this what you guys do for fun in medical school?" All fifteen doctors began to laugh out loud. One was bent at the waist with laughter. I was relieved to be free of the tube, but to me it was no laughing matter.

I was discharged the next day, a Thursday, and this time I had adult supervision for a couple of days before I was left alone. The surgeon instructed me to not lift anything heavy and to not exercise or exert myself, orders that would remain in place for the next four years. By Saturday evening, I was alone again. I felt a tickle in my nose and sneezed hard three times. Then my nose began to bleed as if I'd broken it. I stood at my bathroom sink for almost two hours trying to stop the flow of blood. I pinched my nose and pressed on my upper gum but none of the tricks helped stop the flow of blood. After twenty minutes or so, I'd clear out my sinuses and start over. About forty-five minutes into this ordeal, I began to have trouble seeing out of my eyes. When I looked in the mirror, I saw blood trickling down my cheek. It had flowed up the tube and into my eyes. I looked like I belonged on a heavy metal album cover from the 1980s. The oxygen that they had been pumping into my nose, trying to keep me alive just a few days prior, had left a dried-out hole in my nose. I would need to get it cauterized, but on this Saturday night, I was all my myself. I couldn't let go of my nose long enough to get dressed or get my phone. If I let go of my nose, I bled all over everything. In the end, I got the bleeding to stop, but my bathroom looked like a murder scene. I don't know why I didn't panic. I just tried to stay as calm as I could. I eventually got a shower and cleaned up my bathroom before going to bed, but my ordeal with cancer was just beginning.

Radiation

Once my thyroid gland was removed doctors could physically see what was going on. I had a 2.5 cm tumor on each side of my thyroid. Samples were taken and tests were performed, and I was diagnosed with stage four papillary and stage four follicular cancer. Because the cancers had spread into the surrounding capillaries and into the lymph system, I was going to need radiation.

Due to the tests performed in relation to my needing to be intubated, I would have a four-month delay on radiation. When I was told I'd need radiation, I figured I'd get beam radiation like you get at the dentist when they take x-rays. I'd been through this with Sheryl. The hardest part was the drive to the doctor's office. I was shocked into stunned silence when I found out that I would be ingesting a pill that would irradiate my body. I was going to be a walking radioactive popsicle. I was glad I had a few months to prepare.

Growing up a child of the cold war, I have been aware of the existential threat to society posed by the nuclear power we called the Soviet Union. At any given minute, they could launch nuclear weapons, and society as we know it would suddenly halt. I'd seen movies about it on TV, and I'd read about it in school. Later, in my history classes, I'd teach about the horrible effects on the people of Japan as they suffered from two little bombs dropped on two cities. I'd presented lectures on nuclear war, and I'd shown the civil defense movies about how to prepare for a nuclear blast. Nuclear energy and war and its aftermath were engraved in my mind. Now I was going to ingest irradiated iodine. Visions from both a civil defense movie and a disaster movie filled my mind, and I contemplated the effects of passing a radioactive gas cloud. I'd fart and a young boy from the movie would duck and cover before riding his bike like a squirrel on crack to get away from the radioactive cloud flowing towards him. I struggled to accept this. I needed time to accept my new reality and what it would mean.

As I neared my radiation period of isolation, I was placed on a special diet. This diet would allow me to absorb the most nuclear waste, and the treatment would get the best results. People that I knew from my church decided I needed meals while I was in isolation. I wasn't given a choice. They showed up at my door and much food was delivered. The problem was that I really didn't have any use for it. It sat for months in my freezer before a failure of the old deep freeze meant I had to dispose of all the thawed food.

What bothered me most about the meals was that I had been asked about the food, and when I declined the food, it was delivered anyway. No one wanted to hear what my real needs were: that my son would need many play dates with other kids while I was isolated. Instead, they made themselves feel good by bringing over the food. Once again, I felt like I was asking for a chance to get a cup of coffee and was being refused. My words had been ignored again.

Time passed quickly. On my assigned date I reported to a hospital in the greater Portland area. I was escorted to a conference room for what was called counseling. What it turned out to be was an explanation of an entire list of things I couldn't do. For example, I couldn't go to an airport or train station, or I would be arrested. I was quarantined. If anyone did visit, they were to sit at least twenty-five feet from me. I was instructed on how to get rid of waste and anything I touched. I was also told I needed to drink 16oz of water every hour and make myself use the restroom hourly.

It took about six hours for the radiation to take effect, and then I was done for. I was so tired, all I wanted to do was to sleep. I set a timer on my phone to wake me every sixty minutes. I would not get any good REM sleep for the next week. I would slowly slog through each day. Time stood still, and I had no reference to the time of day other than the light outside.

As a part of the preparation for getting your body ready for radiation, you are given two shots that remove all thyroid stimulating hormone from your body. The result is you feel sick, almost like you have the flu. An acquaintance drove me to my first radiation treatment. He laughed about his exposure rate the entire hour drive to my house. If he hadn't driven me, I don't know if I'd have made it. The results of the prep were as bad as the treatment. Because the endocrine system is manipulated in preparation for radiation, your body is completely out of synch. You feel terrible for weeks and you gain massive amounts of weight. It doesn't matter what you do, you will gain weight. In my case I put on over seventy-five pounds, and just about the time I returned to my starting weight, it was time for another round of radiation. Only this time I didn't have any help. Somehow, I managed to get to the hospital and home again. A couple of times I almost drove off the road. When I asked around, all my friends were busy, and family had to work. I did have a friend volunteer to drive me to my follow up appointment after my second round of radiation. He was a huge blessing.

Three months after my second round of radiation I was supposed to have a follow up ultrasound, but it was postponed for six months due to covid lockdowns. I knew I had something growing in my neck but couldn't get in to see a doctor to get it checked out. Time passed. January turned into July, and I was finally administered the ultrasound and later biopsies were taken. More tumors were found along with cancer in more lymph nodes. I would need to have most of the lymph nodes removed from the right side of my neck. The surgeon would also remove the tumors that were growing in the thyroid bed. Blood tests would follow, and a follow up ultrasound revealed that a cancerous lymph node would require surgery, but this time, I wouldn't need any follow up procedures. It was a struggle that lasted four years, but I was given a clean bill of health and told I'd need to keep my regularly scheduled check-ups and blood tests. Could the cancer return? It could. Could I require additional surgeries? I sure could. Am I past the worst of it? I think so.

Upon Reflection

WHEN I REFLECT ON MY cancer battle and the span of years between my wife's passing and my initial diagnosis with cancer there are three big differences between the experiences: Differences that took a difficult situation and made it livable. Differences that helped me realize just how difficult the previous years really were. Differences that have helped me measure how much better my life is.

I have some friends, not exceptionally close but more than just acquaintances, who stepped up and helped me when I was in need. These friends helped me get to appointments when driving was difficult or forbidden. They brought me food when I asked because I needed a meal. They encouraged me as only a friend can do. There were some dark days that ended less grey because a friend stopped by to give me a card or send an encouraging text or bring me a cup of coffee. The power of a friendship can be hard to measure, but the results can't be missed.

Family helped carry the burden. Again, there were rides I needed to medical procedures. When I was in the ICU, family was present at my bedside and helped me in more ways than I probably know. They also helped care for Tucker during my hospital stays. Two weeks after a major surgery, I needed to change domiciles. Family all showed up and helped with last minute packing and did the heavy lifting that I wasn't supposed to do. Without their help I wouldn't have been able to complete the move.

I was in the center of the battle. I wasn't trying to defeat a schedule or manipulate food to make a meal. I wasn't at the mercy of a stain remover on my clothes. I was the fight. How I approached each day and my attitude towards my treatment set the attitude for the rest of the day. There were days that demanded all my strength to get through it. I make sure I take all my prescribed meds, and I take as good care of myself as I can. Better health is dependent on me and me alone.

Within a week of being told that I was cancer free and shouldn't need any further treatment, our state began to lessen the covid restrictions. I was overjoyed. I could once again have a social life and entertain others in my home, but I was faced with a challenge: Whom would I invite over? I have been forced to be isolated from other people, not because I have had cancer or covid or that my state had mandatory lock downs. I was isolated because I was a single person. I wanted to have social interactions with others. All my church relationships happened within the walls of the church. I found myself getting very depressed. Where was the second person mentioned in Ecclesiastes. I wanted a second chord, even a third, but I was still as alone as I'd always been. I began to question my situation. Why was I struggling so much to make friends? What was working against me?

A Model to Follow

Where were you on September 19, 2000? Do you remember what you were doing? No peeking on the internet. What was the big story of the day? Eric the Eel. Eric is from the nation of Equatorial Guinea. Through a loophole in the rules, he qualified for an Olympic swimming event he had never actually completed. Prior to his race, he had never actually seen an Olympic-sized swimming pool, let alone swum in one. He had practiced in a hotel pool swimming a few meters at a time before turning around and swimming back to the starting point. In this race, the other two competitors false started leaving Eric all by himself to complete the race.

When the gun sounded, Eric launched himself into Olympic history. Eric swam as fast as he could. Legs flailing and arms paddling like mad. At the turn, he completed a flip turn and pushed off, headed for the finish line, but as he neared the middle of the pool, his already slow pace would falter even more. Some people at pool side wondered if they should jump in and save the competitor from drowning. Eric would not be denied. The crowd, realizing that this was his Olympic moment, rose to their collective feet and cheered for Eric as loudly as they would for the gold medal race. With the building shaking from the noise and the crowd screaming at the top of their lungs, an exhausted Eric finally reached the end of the one hundred meter freestyle race. The crowd continued to cheer for Eric as he rested and regained his strength so he could climb out of the pool. He would claim the title of first place finisher in his heat and would earn the slowest time ever recorded in the Olympics, almost two minutes.

It's exciting to see others overcome the obstacles that keep them from success. It's encouraging to us as humans to cheer others on, except in church life. If someone struggles or has a difficult week, some church people want to throw them out of the church. Their spiritual devotion is questioned, and they are shunned. What I've found is that some people in church would just as soon watch you drown as to help you.

The Dilemma

As I have been writing, I have had conversations with others who are in the same situation that I am in. The people they once considered friends have walked away from the friendship due to the death of a loved one, or a divorce, and like me, they have no friends to help them as they struggle with daily life and responsibilities. As I began to search for answers, I sat down with people I knew who were in similar situations and asked them about their experiences. I was saddened to learn that many people are treated so badly by some people in the church.

Let me share just a few of the stories. One lady was in an abusive marriage. She told the leaders of her church that she was filing for divorce but was told to stay with her marriage. Christian ladies that she considered friends said the same thing. "Why get a divorce? You're still going to have to talk to your ex." The message for this lady was it was wrong to leave an abusive marriage. The underlying message here: We don't care about your well-being. Just stick with your marriage regardless of the consequences.

Another conversation: A gentleman's ex-wife was going around to people in the church and lying, saying he was cheating on her. The reverse was actually the truth, and she was the one cheating and wanting out of the marriage. No one took the time to double check her story and assumed she was telling the truth, but ten years later, his second wife, a lady he had no contact with until after his first marriage ended, is still viewed at the cause of the breakup.

Another man was at work and his wife decided that she wanted to reset her life, so she lied to the church leaders. They all met him at his home after work and gave him the ultimatum to clear out his belongings. No options were offered. Just get out of the house and the church.

When I asked these people if I could spend a few minutes of their time for a conversation, I told them I would be done within thirty minutes. I knew they were busy and that their time was valuable, but as conversations began to develop every single person talked for more than thirty minutes. Some conversations lasted over two hours. These people were hurting just like I was and wanted to talk about the hurt and distrust shown them. In this we shared a commonality.

The people in these stories are real people with whom I have the privilege of regular weekly contact. They have fears and struggles just like everyone else, but they have also been shunned and rejected from people in the church. Some have been rebuked by church leadership. Some of them have been told they needed to step aside from ministry opportunities that they were serving in. All have been judged and found guilty of committing a sin, and no one can talk to them anymore. They have been abandoned by the people of the church. If these people were Eric the Eel from earlier, Eric would have drowned because the crowd would have thrown rocks at him instead of cheering him on. And we wonder why people leave the church and turn from God?

Single People, YUK!

I understand why people distance themselves from the newly single person. It's messy. What should we talk about? What if I'm friends with the other spouse in a divorce situation? What if the person I'm shunning isn't following God the way I think they should? The list goes on and on with a million and one excuses, but all the while the newly single person is left alone with no one to help them navigate daily life. Remember, this isn't limited to divorced people. I am single because I'm a widower. I have two people with whom I get together outside of the church walls. Except for these two people, I went over six years without an invitation to get together with someone from my church. Why? Do people not want to invite me to get together with them because they're afraid they might say something wrong, or do they think that I still have friends? Where is the disconnect occurring? Why are people not getting the care they need?

When someone loses a loved one or gets a divorce, their entire world gets turned upside down and shaken. Their entire existence is reset. They now have to do things that the spouse always did. I always cleaned the gutters on my house. The chore was never on my wife's to-do list. The newly-single person has to make decisions that would normally require advise from someone close like a spouse only they no longer have a spouse or a friend to fill in for the spouse. When is a good time to get a new car? Or replace a major kitchen appliance? Where is the help for a person in need? I don't think that help exists. If you are a divorced person or had a spouse die, you might as well have leprosy. You are not allowed to seek help from other church members, and if you do buddy up with other single people, then rumors are started as if you're back in junior high school again. The rumors have romantically attached me to at least six different ladies in my church. I have dated exactly zero of them, but that doesn't stop a good rumor from being shared.

Let's Get It Fixed

After a few conversations, I realized that the problem is bigger than I. I wasn't the only person left alone to fend for themselves. I realized that the people I was talking with at church were all isolated by the church. I also realized that even though I was specifically dealing with being a single parent, I was also a person fighting cancer, and my earlier predicament hadn't changed anything. A couple of times I asked for help from a person whom I had at one time called a friend. He was too busy to help me out for just a few minutes. I was still being shunned and ostracized by the people who told me they were praying for me and supporting me in any way I needed help.

The question remained, whom would I invite over to my house? Whom would I socialize with? Whom would I begin to rely on to cheer me on in life, or carry my burden? I realized that I needed to make friends with the people who had been hurt not just by life events but by the same church I claimed to attend. The next question I asked myself was why these people should trust me to treat them any differently than the way they had been treated.

Wanna Get Some Coffee?

My first experience was in basic training. We were receiving assignments to our next training locations, and some of the guys were being separated from good friends, so they were making commitments about getting together in the future. A couple of guys went so far as to tear a large denomination bill into two parts with each person taking half and making a commitment to get together for a celebration when training was completed. Later I would learn that this was more common than I imagined. I was in the middle of a conversation with one of my divorced friends, and we were talking about community and how we build community. I told him of this practice and how life in 2021 is so focused on internet apps that it would be hard to do this anymore. No one hands out gift certificates made of paper. He suggested that I give them a coffee mug. My brain began to process, and old thoughts moved to the front of my mind.

A few years previously, a friend had suggested I use paint pens on a white mug as an illustrative point for teaching writing in class. I figured I would use this method to further the community building and friendship making in my life. I started to gather my supplies, but I soon realized that I lack any arts and crafts skills. No matter. I pushed forward. First, I purchased plain white coffee mugs and paint pens. I colored half of the coffee mugs with my name, and each of the people I would be praying for had their name placed on a mug, too. I then distributed the mugs with a bag of coffee and explained how the process worked. I told them that every time I used the mug with their name on it, I would pray for them. I asked if they would do the same for me. To my surprise they were overjoyed at the prospect of what I offered. Big smiles were offered along with a reassuring "absolutely" or "this is so cool!" A few days later, I received a picture of an empty plate and a coffee mug. I was told that I had been prayed for and was considered a part of the breakfast mealtime that day. What developed over the next few weeks was that a bunch of isolated outcasts began to pray for each other. We are now a part of each other's lives and need to stay in touch to best know how to pray for each other. We are getting more closely connected than ever before.

Epilogue

Evaluation

"HAPPY MOTHER'S DAY!" SHE EXCLAIMED with a great big smile. It was Mother's Day 2021 and a longtime acquaintance and new friend came up to me and gave me a big hug. I was surprised and speechless. I didn't consider myself a mom, but as I look back over the last decade, I am forced to accept my new paradigm and that fact that at times I am a mom. I realize that I have been in a constant struggle each and every day, first by helping my wife battle cancer and then caring for her as that battle was lost. My life changed and time was measured by how well I survived each day as the parent of a young boy, learned how to cook and run a house, then later as a person battling my own cancer. And some days I've filled the role of Mom. As I have come out of my cancer treatment, I have struggled with where I am in this world. Do I have any friends? What is my relationship with those who call themselves my friend but only mouth empty words and whose actions are nonexistent? I contrast this with recent events.

I was very sick with covid. As I began week number two, and my lungs became affected with the disease, a friend who lives a long distance from me and was checking in on me, called a family member and got me some care so I could begin to see an end to my covid illness. Then a few days later as I was nearing the end of week number two, I got a simple text message.

My Mother's Day friend had been on vacation and this day was her first day back to work. She had many reasons to not text me and check in on me. She had been three thousand miles from home and had many emails waiting her answer at work, but she took the time at seven in the morning to text me just to see how I was doing. As I read her text, I began to cry. I realized I was cared for. Something I hadn't had in years. People cared enough about me to check on me even when it wasn't convenient. A friend put action to their words. When she said she was my friend she followed up with an action: she checked in on me even when she had many tasks to complete on this day after vacation. It was just a simple text, but that simple text was such an emotional boost to me after having a high fever for two weeks. It was the emotional hug I needed to continue my fight.

There was a time in my life when I thought I had many friends, but they seemed to vanish after my wife passed away. For many years I had no one to check on me. No one texted or called. I nearly died because I couldn't see the large blood clot forming on my neck and closing off my windpipe. No one was in close contact with me. Now I have just a couple people who check in on me, but I am so blessed by these few. I know that if I need anything, they are just a simple text or phone call away. I know that if I have a problem, they will drop whatever they are doing and rush to my aid even if it means leaving work or getting on a plane and flying halfway across the North American continent. The comfort of their texts or phone calls extends to the very core of my soul. My life is now richer, fuller, better, and they know that I would do the same for them if the need were ever to arise.

I have a friend who I now invite over for burgers on the Q! Her boys and my son are friends and enjoy playing video games together. Card games and card tricks are always a part of the evening fun. The events of the last decade have been hard. Many sharp edges have been worn smooth, and I no longer take the actions of a friend for granted. Occasionally in my mind I find myself wandering back to the church parking lot in the fall off 2013. I am standing alongside the car of the person who at the time, I referred to as my closest friend, and I hear his voice, "You can expect that all the people who have been supporting you these last few months will drift away, and you'll find that your support network pretty much doesn't exist."

And I give thanks daily for the true friends that I now have.

References

1. All scripture The Holy Bible NIV, California, Harper Collins 2021

2. Lewis, C.S., Editor Hooper, Walter. Present Concerns. New York, Harper One, 2017.

3. Greitens, Eric. Resilience: Hard Won Wisdom for Living a Better Life. New York, Houghton Mifflin Harcourt Publishing, 2015